Unlocking Altcoin Potential

Emerging Cryptocurrencies: The Next Frontier of Digital Assets

Max Sterling

Table of Contents

INTRODUCTION

The introduction of cryptocurrencies ushered in a period of profound change experienced across the digital environment. With the advent of Bitcoin, a concept that was formerly confined to a particular portion of the population has now evolved into a vast and complex ecosystem consisting of decentralized applications, blockchain technology, and digital assets. An intriguing area known as "altcoins" may be found at the very center of this ecosystem. Altcoins are alternative cryptocurrencies that have developed to compete with and complement the pioneer cryptocurrency, Bitcoin.

In this e-book, titled "Unlocking Altcoin Potential: Emerging Cryptocurrencies- The Next Frontier of Digital Assets," we go deeply into the dynamic realm of emerging cryptocurrencies and the world of altcoins. These alternative coins are becoming powerful contenders as the cryptocurrency environment extends beyond the limitations of Bitcoin. They offer innovative solutions, applications, and investment opportunities. We hope that by the time you finish reading this e-book, you will have a thorough grasp of the altcoin universe, including its technologies, investment potentials, and the broader implications that altcoins hold for the future of finance and technology.

Bitcoin, the first cryptocurrency, demonstrated the viability of a decentralized, digital currency system that could function independently of the traditional intermediaries typically used in financial transactions. However, as blockchain technology, which forms the basis of cryptocurrencies, continued to progress, it became abundantly evident that the possibilities stretched far beyond those of a simple digital currency. Altcoins are a varied spectrum of cryptocurrencies that build upon the foundation laid by Bitcoin by offering additional features, capabilities, and use cases. They can be thought of as a world unto itself.

A spirit of innovation drives the cryptocurrency community, and the rise of altcoins is not merely a phenomenon; instead, it is a monument to that mentality. In this e-book, we take a detailed look at the notion of emerging cryptocurrencies, which are defined as digital assets that are making steps forward due to the implementation of innovative technology, consensus mechanisms, and applications. These up-and-coming cryptocurrencies have the potential to transform sectors, give consumers more power, and challenge the norms that are now in place. Examples include interoperability solutions and smart contracts.

Placing investment into alternative coins is a risky business requiring much knowledge, investigation, and planning. We will walk you through the complexities of investing in altcoins throughout this e-book. In this e-book, we discuss risk assessment, fundamental and technical analysis, and offer some insights into building a diversified altcoin portfolio. In addition, we discuss the regulatory environment that affects these investments, making it possible for you to make well-informed choices by arming you with the information you need.

Although the possibility for financial benefits is a significant factor, the utility and influence of altcoins extend far beyond the realm of finance. This e-book focuses on real-world applications of new cryptocurrencies and provides examples of their use. These alternative cryptocurrencies play a vital role in molding the future of technology, art, entertainment, and other fields. This is the case regardless of whether they are redefining ownership with Non-Fungible Tokens (NFTs) or redefining finance through Decentralized Finance (DeFi).

As we progress across the landscape of alternative coins, we are aware that this terrain is not devoid of obstacles in any way. Several considerations need to be taken into account, including regulatory uncertainty, technical challenges, and volatile market conditions. In the last few chapters of this e-book, we delve into these challenges and provide some insights into the ways in which the alternative coin ecosystem may develop and adjust in response to shifting conditions.

The age of alternative coins and emerging forms of digital currency has begun, and the opportunities it presents are practically endless. You will acquire the information and tools necessary to navigate this thrilling landscape with the help of this e-book, which will serve as your guide. The e-book "Unlocking Altcoin Potential: Emerging Cryptocurrencies- The Next Frontier of Digital Assets" is your guide to understanding and embracing this ever-changing world, regardless of whether you're an investor looking for new opportunities, a technologist curious about blockchain innovation, or simply someone intrigued by the potential of the digital future. This e-book serves as your compass to understanding and embracing this dynamic realm.

Therefore, let's begin on this journey together and explore the ever-expanding frontiers of altcoins and emerging forms of digital currency.

CHAPTER I

Understanding Altcoins

Definition of altcoins and their role in the crypto landscape

In cryptocurrencies' vast and ever-evolving realm, the term "altcoin" emerges as a pivotal concept that extends beyond its succinct label. Altcoins, short for "alternative coins," encompass a diverse range of digital currencies that occurred in the wake of Bitcoin, the pioneering cryptocurrency. While Bitcoin holds the distinction of being the first decentralized digital currency, altcoins have since emerged to offer variations, innovations, and alternatives to the foundational principles set forth by Bitcoin. These alternative cryptocurrencies showcase the inherent flexibility of blockchain technology and the potential for myriad applications beyond simple peer-to-peer digital transactions.

At its core, an altcoin is a cryptocurrency that operates on a blockchain similar to that of Bitcoin but with modifications, improvements, or distinct features that set it apart. These modifications can encompass various aspects, including consensus mechanisms, transaction speeds, privacy features, and utility-driven functionalities. By embracing alterations to Bitcoin's original protocol, altcoins have become laboratories of experimentation, embodying the innovative spirit of the crypto community and driving the evolution of digital assets.

The role of altcoins within the broader crypto landscape is multifaceted and evolving. One of the primary roles of altcoins is to address limitations or perceived shortcomings in Bitcoin's design. For instance, Bitcoin's proof-of-work consensus mechanism has been criticized for its energy-intensive nature and potential scalability issues. In response, altcoins have introduced alternative consensus mechanisms like proof-of-stake, which require participants to show ownership of a certain number of coins to validate transactions. This innovation reduces

energy consumption and addresses scalability concerns, allowing more transactions to be processed in a shorter time frame.

Furthermore, altcoins have pioneered the introduction of specialized functionalities that cater to specific use cases. Take Ethereum, for instance, which is often considered the quintessential altcoin. Smart contracts are agreements that may execute themselves and have their conditions encoded directly into code. Ethereum was the initial blockchain platform to introduce the notion of smart contracts. This innovation enabled the creation of decentralized applications (DApps) that go beyond simple transactions, enabling functionalities such as automated asset exchanges, decentralized finance (DeFi) protocols, and even non-fungible tokens (NFTs), revolutionizing ownership and representation of digital assets.

Altcoins also play a vital role in diversifying the cryptocurrency market, offering investors a broader range of investment options. While Bitcoin remains a foundational and sought-after investment, altcoins provide opportunities for investors to allocate funds into projects with unique value propositions and growth potentials. This diversification can potentially mitigate risks associated with investing solely in one cryptocurrency, spreading exposure across different assets and technologies.

However, it's important to note that the altcoin landscape has challenges and considerations. The rapid proliferation of altcoins has led to concerns about oversaturation and the potential for low-quality projects or outright scams. When navigating the altcoin market, investors need to proceed with extreme caution and conduct extensive research because not all projects are made equal. In order to make educated decisions regarding investments, it is necessary to conduct exhaustive study, have a grasp of the underlying technology of each altcoin, and evaluate the credibility of the development team.

In conclusion, altcoins represent a dynamic and transformative force within cryptocurrency. These alternative cryptocurrencies exemplify the adaptability of blockchain technology, allowing for continuous experimentation and innovation. By addressing limitations, introducing novel functionalities, and diversifying investment options, altcoins contribute significantly to shaping the future of digital assets. However, navigating the altcoin landscape requires vigilance and discernment to differentiate between valuable projects and potential pitfalls. As the crypto ecosystem continues to evolve, altcoins remain a captivating arena where new possibilities emerge and the boundaries of technology are continuously pushed.

Historical context: the rise of Bitcoin and the need for alternative cryptocurrencies

The introduction of Bitcoin in 2009 is considered to be the year that marked the beginning of the digital currency revolution. Created by an individual or group under the pseudonym Satoshi Nakamoto, Bitcoin introduced a revolutionary concept: a decentralized digital currency that operated without intermediaries such as banks or governments. This groundbreaking innovation began a new era in finance and technology, paving the way for the rise of alternative cryptocurrencies, often called "altcoins."

In the early days, Bitcoin's significance was not fully grasped. It was primarily perceived as a novel experiment, intriguing to a niche community of cryptography enthusiasts, libertarians, and computer scientists. Its initial value was negligible, and its potential impact on the traditional financial system was largely underestimated. However, as the years unfolded, Bitcoin's core principles began to resonate far beyond its initial circle of supporters.

A growing disillusionment with the traditional financial system fueled Bitcoin's rise. The worldwide financial crisis of 2008 brought to light the vulnerabilities of centralized institutions and the influence that these organizations have on the financial sovereignty of individuals. Bitcoin emerged as an antidote to these concerns, offering a decentralized, borderless, and censorship-resistant form of value exchange. This allure, combined with its innovative blockchain technology, propelled Bitcoin into the mainstream conversation, attracting tech-savvy enthusiasts and investors, speculators, and institutions seeking to diversify their portfolios.

Yet, even as Bitcoin gained prominence, it became evident that the original cryptocurrency had its limitations. One of the most pressing issues was scalability. The Bitcoin network's design, which emphasized security through proof-of-work consensus, resulted in slower transaction speeds and higher fees as the network's usage grew. This bottleneck hindered Bitcoin's potential as a practical medium of exchange for everyday transactions, leading to the emergence of "altcoins" that sought to address these shortcomings.

Litecoin, introduced in 2011 by Charlie Lee, is one of the earliest successful altcoins. It aimed to address Bitcoin's scalability issues by employing a different hashing algorithm and reducing block confirmation times. This resulted in faster transaction processing and a blockchain capable of handling higher transaction volumes. Litecoin's success demonstrated the viability of alternative approaches within the cryptocurrency space and spurred the development of numerous other altcoins, each with its unique features and goals.

Furthermore, altcoins filled important niches that Bitcoin did not directly cater to. For instance, Ripple (now known as XRP) focused on facilitating fast and low-cost cross-border transactions, targeting the inefficiencies of traditional remittance systems. Namecoin aimed to decentralize the domain name system, reducing the reliance on centralized authorities for website address allocation. These examples highlighted how altcoins could address specific industry challenges and pioneer innovative solutions beyond simple peer-to-peer digital cash.

As the cryptocurrency ecosystem expanded, the term "altcoin" began encompassing an ever-growing variety of digital assets. Some altcoins sought to enhance privacy and anonymity, addressing concerns about traceability on public blockchains. Others introduced novel consensus mechanisms like proof-of-stake, which reduced energy consumption and improved scalability. The rapid development of altcoins underscored the dynamic nature of the crypto landscape, characterized by continuous innovation, experimentation, and adaptation.

In conclusion, the rise of Bitcoin marked a pivotal moment in history, sparking a paradigm shift in how we perceive and utilize currency. As the shortcomings of Bitcoin became apparent, the need for alternative cryptocurrencies emerged. Altcoins, borne out of a desire to address scalability, efficiency, and specific use cases, have diversified and enriched the cryptocurrency ecosystem. While Bitcoin remains the bedrock of the digital currency revolution, altcoins have proven to be catalysts for innovation, pushing the boundaries of blockchain technology and challenging the conventions of traditional finance. The historical context surrounding the rise of Bitcoin underscores the cyclical nature of innovation—where a groundbreaking idea begets the need for evolution and diversification, leading to a cascade of innovation in the pursuit of a decentralized future.

Categories of altcoins: forks, tokens, stablecoins, privacy coins, etc.

The evolution of cryptocurrencies has given rise to a diverse array of digital assets, collectively known as altcoins. These alternative cryptocurrencies, born out of the need for innovation and specialization, have expanded beyond the confines of Bitcoin's pioneering blueprint. Altcoins can be categorized into distinct groups, each with its own unique features, functionalities, and purposes. In this section, we explore the various categories of altcoins, ranging from forks to tokens, stablecoins, privacy coins, and beyond, shedding light on their significance in the ever-expanding crypto landscape.

One prominent category within the altcoin universe is forks, which can be divided into soft and hard forks. A soft fork involves a backward-compatible upgrade to the existing blockchain protocol, whereas a hard fork results in a permanent divergence from the original blockchain. A prime example of a hard fork is Bitcoin Cash, created in 2017 as an alternative to Bitcoin. Bitcoin Cash aimed to address Bitcoin's scalability limitations by increasing block sizes, allowing more transactions to be processed in each block. This division exemplified how forks can stem from differing visions within the community and provide a platform for experimentation and innovation.

Tokens are another vital category of altcoins that leverage existing blockchain platforms to build upon their infrastructure. Ethereum is the most well-known blockchain for token creation because it was the first blockchain to introduce the notion of smart contracts. Tokens can represent various assets, including digital assets, a utility within a specific ecosystem, or even real-world assets like real estate or commodities. For instance, the rise of decentralized finance (DeFi) platforms led to the creation of numerous tokens representing lending, borrowing, and liquidity provision. Moreover, initial coin offerings (ICOs) facilitated the issuance of tokens as a means of fundraising for innovative projects, illustrating the versatility and democratizing potential of tokenization.

In a landscape marked by extreme price volatility, stablecoins emerged as a practical solution to maintain the benefits of cryptocurrencies while mitigating the risks of value fluctuations. Stablecoins are pegged to external assets like fiat currencies or commodities, ensuring a stable value that facilitates use in everyday transactions, trading, and as a store of value. Tether (USDT), for instance, is pegged to the US Dollar, allowing users to navigate the crypto ecosystem with a stable reference point. The rise of stablecoins also bridged the gap between the traditional financial system and the world of cryptocurrencies, facilitating easier entry for newcomers while enhancing overall market stability.

Privacy coins represent a category of altcoins designed to address the issue of transaction privacy and anonymity, a concern that has gained prominence in the age of blockchain transparency. Coins like Monero (XMR) and Zcash (ZEC) implement advanced cryptographic techniques to obscure transaction details, including sender, receiver, and transaction amount. These coins empower users with a higher degree of financial privacy, contrasting with the pseudonymous nature of Bitcoin transactions. However, the rise of privacy coins has sparked debates about their potential misuse for illicit activities and regulatory challenges related to transaction traceability.

Utility coins, often called "app coins," are native tokens within specific blockchain ecosystems. They are integral to the functionality and operation of decentralized applications (DApps) within their respective platforms. Ethereum's Ether (ETH) is a prime example, as it is used to pay transaction fees and execute smart contracts within the Ethereum network. These coins are not merely speculative assets; they hold practical value within the ecosystems they support, fueling a wide range of decentralized services, from gaming to finance and beyond.

Beyond these primary categories, altcoins continue to push the boundaries of innovation, giving rise to niche categories that address specific challenges or industries. For instance, there are altcoins focused on improving energy efficiency, integrating blockchain with the Internet of Things (IoT), or revolutionizing supply chain management. Each of these altcoins seeks to pioneer solutions for existing problems by harnessing the power of blockchain technology.

In conclusion, the world of altcoins is a dynamic and multifaceted realm extending far beyond Bitcoin's original design. These diverse categories of altcoins—forks, tokens, stablecoins, privacy coins, utility coins, and beyond—illustrate the breadth of innovation and specialization within the cryptocurrency landscape. As altcoins evolve and cater to specific use cases and challenges, they collectively shape the future of finance, technology, and human interaction. The variety and complexity within these categories mirror the ever-adapting nature of blockchain technology and its potential to transform industries, redefine traditional financial paradigms, and foster a decentralized future.

Pros and cons of investing in altcoins

The world of cryptocurrencies extends far beyond the iconic Bitcoin, encompassing a diverse range of digital assets commonly referred to as altcoins. These alternative cryptocurrencies have gained prominence due to their potential for innovation, utility, and investment opportunities. However, with the potential rewards come inherent risks and challenges. In this section, we delve into the pros and cons of investing in altcoins, exploring the opportunities and pitfalls investors must navigate within this dynamic and rapidly evolving landscape.

Diversification is a cornerstone principle of sound investment strategy. Altcoins allow investors to diversify their portfolios beyond traditional asset classes. While

Bitcoin remains a foundational investment, altcoins offer exposure to various use cases, technologies, and market trends. By spreading investments across different altcoins, investors can potentially reduce the impact of poor performance in any single asset, thereby enhancing overall portfolio resilience.

Altcoins are often at the forefront of technological innovation within the blockchain space. Projects like Ethereum introduced smart contracts, enabling the creation of decentralized applications (DApps) that extend beyond simple value transfer. Other altcoins focus on scalability solutions, privacy enhancements, and interoperability, driving the evolution of blockchain technology. Investing in innovative altcoins presents financial opportunities and contributes to developing the broader crypto ecosystem.

Altcoins cater to a wide array of specific use cases and industries. For instance, privacy coins like Monero prioritize transaction anonymity, appealing to users concerned about data privacy. Decentralized finance (DeFi) tokens enable users to participate in lending, borrowing, and yield farming in a decentralized ecosystem. Investing in altcoins aligned with specific niche markets provides an opportunity to support projects addressing real-world challenges.

Early investment in promising altcoins can yield substantial returns as these projects gain adoption and market recognition. Many altcoins have experienced meteoric price rises, particularly during bull market cycles. Those who identify high-potential projects and invest early can capture exponential returns, leveraging the inherent volatility of the cryptocurrency market to their advantage.

The advent of altcoins and initial coin offerings (ICOs) democratized investment opportunities, allowing individuals worldwide to participate in projects at their inception. This accessibility reduced barriers to entry for retail investors and fostered a more inclusive investment landscape. Altcoin investments were no longer the exclusive domain of venture capitalists or institutional players.

The market for cryptocurrencies is notorious for having extremely volatile price levels. While volatility can create opportunities for substantial gains, it also exposes investors to significant risk. Altcoins, especially those in their early stages, are susceptible to sharp and unpredictable price fluctuations driven by market sentiment, regulatory developments, technological challenges, or the performance of the broader crypto market.

The altcoin market operates relatively unregulated, leading to concerns about investor protection and fraudulent activities. Scams, pump-and-dump schemes, and fraudulent projects have been documented, exploiting the lack of regulatory oversight. The absence of clear regulations can expose investors to financial losses and hinder the market's long-term credibility. While

major altcoins may enjoy relatively high liquidity, smaller or less-established altcoins can suffer from limited trading volume. Due to the lack of liquidity in the market, it can be difficult to execute large trades without having a substantial effect on the pricing. Not all altcoins are accessible on all cryptocurrency exchanges, potentially limiting investors' ability to buy or sell specific assets.

The altcoin landscape is saturated with projects vying for attention and adoption. While some altcoins successfully carve out their niches and gain user support, many projects struggle to achieve sustainable growth. The competitive nature of the market and the emergence of new projects can overshadow existing ones, leading to challenges in maintaining relevance and long-term sustainability.

Altcoin investments are subject to technical risks related to the underlying blockchain technology and the project's development team. Security vulnerabilities, software bugs, or flaws in smart contracts can lead to severe consequences, including hacking incidents and value loss. Moreover, the success of an altcoin depends on the team's ability to deliver on promises and continuously update the project's technology.
While vibrant and innovative, the altcoin market is relatively young compared to traditional financial markets. As a result, it is susceptible to manipulation, speculative trading, and sudden shifts in market sentiment. Lack of historical data and market maturity can complicate accurate price prediction and investment decision-making.

Investing in altcoins presents a dual-edged opportunity with potential rewards and inherent risks. Diversifying portfolios, innovating, and accessing niche markets are enticing advantages. However, the high volatility, lack of regulation, limited liquidity, competition, and technical risks underscore the challenges of altcoin investments. Successful navigation of the altcoin landscape demands thorough research, risk management strategies, and a clear understanding of personal investment goals and risk tolerance. As the crypto ecosystem continues to evolve, altcoins remain a captivating arena where investors can either thrive on the potential for innovation or encounter the pitfalls of an emerging and dynamic market.

CHAPTER II

Exploring Emerging Cryptocurrencies

What constitutes an emerging cryptocurrency?

The cryptocurrency landscape is constantly in flux, marked by innovations, disruptions, and the emergence of new digital assets. These nascent cryptocurrencies, often called "emerging cryptocurrencies," bring fresh perspectives, advanced technologies, and novel use cases to the forefront of the blockchain space. In this section, we explore the elements that constitute an emerging cryptocurrency, delving into the key characteristics and factors that differentiate these newcomers from established players like Bitcoin and Ethereum.

One of the primary hallmarks of an emerging cryptocurrency is its emphasis on technological innovation. These new entrants into the crypto arena typically introduce advancements that build upon or diverge from the established blockchain models. For instance, while Bitcoin pioneered decentralized digital currency, emerging cryptocurrencies like Ethereum introduced smart contracts and the ability to build decentralized applications (DApps). These innovative features set emerging cryptocurrencies apart, showcasing their capacity to push the boundaries of blockchain technology.

Emerging cryptocurrencies often arrive on the scene with a clear and unique value proposition that distinguishes them from existing digital assets. This value proposition could encompass improved scalability, enhanced privacy features, interoperability solutions, or targeting specific industries like supply chain management or healthcare. The ability to articulate a compelling and distinct use case is crucial in attracting attention and adoption within the competitive cryptocurrency market.

Behind every emerging cryptocurrency lies a dedicated community of developers, enthusiasts, and supporters committed to realizing the project's vision. The development team's expertise, credibility, and transparency play a pivotal role in gaining trust and driving adoption. Additionally, a vibrant and engaged community fosters innovation, provides feedback, and contributes to improving the cryptocurrency's technology and ecosystem.

While emerging cryptocurrencies are often conceptualized within the blockchain and crypto community, their ultimate success hinges on real-world adoption. Cryptocurrencies gain value through their utility and relevance in solving tangible problems. Projects that secure partnerships with established companies, integrate their technology into existing systems, or address pressing industry challenges demonstrate a clear path to adoption and growth.

Navigating the regulatory landscape is a defining aspect of emerging cryptocurrencies. Regulatory clarity or ambiguity can significantly impact the trajectory of a project. Cryptocurrencies that work proactively with regulators, demonstrate compliance with legal requirements, and develop solutions that align with regulatory expectations are better positioned to gain legitimacy and avoid potential obstacles.

Emerging cryptocurrencies must address real market demands and offer solutions that resonate with users. These solutions can range from facilitating cross-border payments and reducing transaction fees to providing decentralized identity verification and improving supply chain transparency. The ability to solve problems or meet unmet needs within existing industries underscores the potential for widespread adoption and utility.

Emerging cryptocurrencies substantiate their viability through technical proof and comprehensive whitepapers. A whitepaper outlines the project's technology, goals, use cases, and plans for development and deployment. This documentation provides potential investors and users with insights into the project's vision, technological underpinnings, and roadmap for achieving its objectives.

Scalability is a critical consideration for emerging cryptocurrencies. As the user base grows and transaction volumes increase, the network must be capable of accommodating these demands without sacrificing performance. Projects that address scalability challenges effectively and demonstrate the potential for achieving network effects are more likely to sustain long-term growth.
A gradual increase in market awareness often marks the emergence of a cryptocurrency. Media coverage, community engagement, and partnerships contribute to raising the cryptocurrency's profile and attracting users, investors, and developers. The growth in adoption and recognition validates the project's viability and potential impact on the blockchain ecosystem.

Emerging cryptocurrencies represent the dynamic spirit of the blockchain space, characterized by innovation, adaptability, and the pursuit of transformative solutions.

A combination of technological advancement, unique value propositions, strong development teams, regulatory awareness, market demand, and scalability considerations defines what constitutes an emerging cryptocurrency. These elements collectively determine whether a project has the potential to disrupt industries, reshape financial paradigms, and contribute to the broader evolution of the cryptocurrency landscape. As the world of cryptocurrencies evolves, emerging projects will continue to captivate the imagination of enthusiasts,
investors, and technologists alike.

Factors driving the emergence of new cryptocurrencies

The cryptocurrency landscape is a rapidly evolving arena characterized by constant innovation, technological breakthroughs, and the emergence of new digital assets. These nascent cryptocurrencies, often called "newcomers" or "altcoins," bring fresh perspectives, solutions, and opportunities to the forefront of the blockchain ecosystem. Behind this wave of innovation lies a multitude of factors that drive the emergence of new cryptocurrencies. In this section, we delve into the key drivers that propel the creation and introduction of these novel digital assets, shedding light on the dynamic forces that shape the ever-evolving crypto landscape.

Technological innovation stands as a foundational driver behind the emergence of new cryptocurrencies. The ongoing evolution of blockchain technology enables developers to experiment with novel concepts, features, and functionalities that extend beyond the capabilities of existing cryptocurrencies. Newcomers often introduce improvements in consensus mechanisms, scalability solutions, privacy features, and interoperability protocols. These innovations attract attention and investment and contribute to the cryptocurrency ecosystem's continuous evolution.

One of the driving factors behind the emergence of new cryptocurrencies is the need to address the limitations of existing digital assets. While pioneers like Bitcoin and Ethereum laid the groundwork for decentralized digital transactions and smart contracts, they have shortcomings. Scalability issues, energy consumption concerns, and privacy challenges have prompted developers to create new solutions that offer better performance, enhanced security, and improved user experience.

New cryptocurrencies often emerge to cater to specific niche use cases and industries. These digital assets target industries such as supply chain management, healthcare, gaming, and identity verification, among others. By focusing on specialized solutions, newcomers can address real-world challenges and provide industries with more efficient, secure, and transparent alternatives to traditional systems. This specialization enhances the value proposition of these cryptocurrencies and attracts users seeking tailored solutions.

Market trends, including changes in user preferences and industry dynamics, influence the emergence of new cryptocurrencies. The rise of decentralized finance (DeFi) platforms, non-fungible tokens (NFTs), and other trends has sparked the creation of cryptocurrencies designed to capitalize on these trends. Developers aim to tap into growing markets and user demands, offering digital assets that align with emerging paradigms and market expectations.

The ethos of decentralization and democratization inherent in the cryptocurrency space drives the creation of new digital assets. Developers seek to challenge centralized control and empower individuals with ownership and control over their digital assets and data. By introducing new cryptocurrencies, creators contribute to the broader goal of creating a decentralized and open financial system that empowers individuals and reduces reliance on traditional intermediaries.

Emerging cryptocurrencies often begin as grassroots initiatives led by passionate developers and community members. These projects gain traction through community-driven efforts, collaboration, and open-source development. The decentralized nature of blockchain technology allows individuals worldwide to contribute to developing, improving, and promoting new cryptocurrencies, fostering a sense of ownership and engagement.

The potential for financial gain through investment and speculation plays a significant role in driving the emergence of new cryptocurrencies. Investors seek opportunities to capitalize on the growth potential of new projects during their early stages. Initial coin offerings (ICOs) and token sales offer a means for projects to raise funds and gain initial support from the investor community, further incentivizing the creation of new cryptocurrencies.

Competition in cryptocurrency encourages developers to create digital assets that stand out through differentiation and innovation. To gain a competitive edge, newcomers often introduce features that set them apart from existing cryptocurrencies. This competition fosters a cycle of continuous improvement and innovation, driving the broader advancement of blockchain technology.

The accessibility of blockchain technology and open-source development tools has democratized the creation of new cryptocurrencies. As a result, a more comprehensive range of individuals and teams can participate in creating digital assets, leading to a diverse array of projects with unique goals and features. This technological democratization encourages innovation and diversity within the cryptocurrency ecosystem.

The emergence of new cryptocurrencies contributes to the ongoing redefinition of the financial landscape. Cryptocurrencies challenge traditional financial systems and offer alternatives prioritizing efficiency, transparency, and inclusivity. The desire to shape the future of finance by introducing new means of value exchange and financial services serves as a driving force for developing and introducing novel cryptocurrencies.

The emergence of new cryptocurrencies is driven by a multitude of factors that span technological innovation, market trends, user demands, decentralization principles, and investment opportunities. Developers and teams within the blockchain space leverage these factors to create digital assets that push the boundaries of technology, address limitations, cater to specific use cases, and contribute to the broader evolution of the cryptocurrency ecosystem. As the landscape continues to evolve, the dynamic interplay of these driving forces will shape the trajectory of the crypto space, fueling continuous innovation and reimagining the possibilities of the digital age.

Case studies of successful emerging cryptocurrencies (e.g., Ethereum, Cardano, Solana)

The cryptocurrency landscape is teeming with innovation as emerging cryptocurrencies introduce groundbreaking technologies, novel use cases, and transformative solutions. Among the many projects, a few standout success stories have garnered widespread attention and adoption. In this section, we delve into three notable case studies—Ethereum, Cardano, and Solana—exploring their journey from inception to prominence and uncovering the key factors that have contributed to their success within the dynamic and competitive crypto ecosystem.

Ethereum, launched in 2015 by Vitalik Buterin, represents a paradigm shift in the blockchain landscape. While Bitcoin was responsible for popularizing the idea of a decentralized digital currency, Ethereum is credited with revolutionizing the industry by facilitating the development of smart contracts and decentralized apps (DApps). Smart contracts are self-executing agreements with predefined rules directly written into code. This innovation transformed the potential applications of blockchain technology beyond simple transactions. Ethereum's success can be attributed to several factors. First, its visionary founder, Vitalik Buterin, recognized the limitations of Bitcoin and sought to create a platform that could support a wide range of use cases. Second, Ethereum's strong development community and open-source nature encouraged collaboration, attracting talented developers to contribute to the project's growth. Third, the Ethereum Virtual Machine (EVM), a decentralized computing environment, made it easier for developers to build and deploy DApps.

Furthermore, Ethereum's successful initial coin offering (ICO) in 2014 provided the necessary funding to realize its ambitious goals. Ethereum's Ether (ETH) token serves as a medium of exchange within the platform and a store of value. The demand for Ether grew as DApps and ICOs proliferated, driving its price upward.

Despite its success, Ethereum faced scalability challenges due to its proof-of-work consensus mechanism. The Ethereum community is actively transitioning to Ethereum 2.0, an upgrade that introduces a proof-of-stake consensus mechanism and scalability improvements. This transition highlights Ethereum's commitment to continuous innovation and adaptation in response to emerging challenges.

Cardano, launched in 2017 by Charles Hoskinson, is a case study combining rigorous research and scientific principles with blockchain technology. The project's goal is to create a third-generation blockchain platform that addresses the scalability, interoperability, and sustainability issues faced by previous generations.

Cardano's approach revolves around a foundation of peer-reviewed research and academic collaboration. This scientific rigor sets Cardano apart and contributes to its credibility within the blockchain space. The project is divided into phases, with each stage introducing specific improvements. For instance, Cardano's Shelley phase introduced staking and a proof-of-stake consensus mechanism, allowing participants to earn rewards by holding and staking its native cryptocurrency, ADA.

Cardano's focus on peer-reviewed research, transparency, and scalability solutions has attracted attention from the crypto community and academia. The project's emphasis on long-term viability, sustainable governance, and scalability underscores its commitment to addressing the challenges faced by previous blockchain platforms.

Solana, launched in 2020 by Anatoly Yakovenko, is a case study tackling the scalability challenge plaguing many blockchain platforms. Solana's innovative approach focuses on achieving high throughput and low latency, enabling the platform to quickly process a high volume of transactions.

Solana introduces a unique combination of technologies, including a proof-of-history consensus mechanism that orders events in the blockchain, facilitating faster consensus among nodes. Additionally, Solana's proof-of-stake consensus mechanism enhances energy efficiency and reduces the environmental impact of blockchain operations. These features make Solana well-suited for hosting high-performance DApps, including decentralized finance (DeFi) platforms, non-fungible token (NFT) marketplaces, and gaming applications.

Solana's success can be attributed to its emphasis on scalability, performance, and fostering an ecosystem of projects and developers. Its ability to handle many transactions while maintaining low fees has attracted investors, developers, and users' attention. Solana's rapid growth and adoption underscore the demand for blockchain platforms capable of supporting high-performance applications.

The case studies of Ethereum, Cardano, and Solana provide valuable insights into the factors driving emerging cryptocurrencies' success. Ethereum's introduction of smart contracts and DApps, Cardano's scientific approach and focus on research, and Solana's emphasis on scalability and performance showcase diverse strategies for achieving prominence within the competitive crypto landscape.

These projects capitalized on visionary leadership, technological innovation, community engagement, and strategic positioning. Ethereum's pioneering role in expanding blockchain's use cases, Cardano's commitment to scientific principles, and Solana's focus on high-performance applications highlight the myriad paths that can lead to success in emerging cryptocurrencies.

As the cryptocurrency ecosystem evolves, these case studies inspire other projects seeking to make their mark. The stories of Ethereum, Cardano, and Solana remind us that success in the blockchain space requires a combination of technological excellence, clear vision, community support, and adaptability to address the evolving challenges and opportunities that define the future of blockchain technology.

Challenges faced by emerging cryptocurrencies

The cryptocurrency landscape is a dynamic and ever-evolving arena characterized by innovation, disruption, and the continuous emergence of new digital assets. While these emerging cryptocurrencies bring fresh ideas, technological advancements, and unique value propositions, they also encounter many challenges that shape their journey from inception to prominence. In this section, we explore the significant challenges emerging cryptocurrencies face, shedding light on the complexities and obstacles that must be navigated within the competitive and rapidly changing crypto ecosystem.

One of the foremost challenges confronting emerging cryptocurrencies is the intense market competition. The sheer number of projects vying for attention and adoption creates a crowded landscape where standing out becomes a daunting task. Newcomers must establish unique value propositions that differentiate them from established players and other emerging projects. Failure to articulate a compelling reason for users and investors to choose a specific cryptocurrency can result in obscurity and limited adoption.

Technological development lies at the heart of any successful cryptocurrency project. However, emerging cryptocurrencies often face challenges in creating and refining their technology to meet user demands and market expectations. Overcoming scalability issues, optimizing consensus mechanisms, and ensuring robust security are crucial but intricate tasks. Additionally, implementing innovative features while balancing usability, safety, and performance requires meticulous engineering and continuous iteration.

Emerging cryptocurrencies face a significant challenge in the form of a complex regulatory landscape that must be navigated. Regulatory frameworks vary across jurisdictions, and the lack of clear guidelines can hinder project development and adoption. For instance, the lack of clarity on whether a particular cryptocurrency would be categorized as a security or a commodity might have an effect on fundraising efforts and market positioning. Projects prioritizing regulatory compliance and transparency are better positioned to gain legitimacy and avoid potential legal issues.

Security vulnerabilities pose a critical threat to emerging cryptocurrencies and their ecosystems. Malicious actors target new projects due to their potential vulnerabilities and limited track record. It is absolutely necessary to carry out stringent security audits, vulnerability assessments, and penetration testing in order to locate weaknesses and solve them before they can be exploited. Ensuring the security of smart contracts, wallet infrastructure, and consensus mechanisms is paramount to building trust among users and investors.

Achieving widespread adoption and building network effects are significant challenges for emerging cryptocurrencies. Users and investors are naturally drawn to projects with established user bases and vibrant communities. Newcomers must overcome the "chicken-and-egg" problem, wherein users are reluctant to adopt a cryptocurrency with limited use cases, while developers are hesitant to build applications for a platform with limited users. Projects that can bootstrap adoption and demonstrate utility quickly gain an advantage.

It is absolutely necessary for the development of emerging cryptocurrencies to have a community that is vibrant and active. A supportive community contributes to the development, adoption, and the project's overall success. However, building and nurturing a community requires time, effort, and effective communication. Establishing transparency, providing regular updates, and fostering engagement through forums, social media, and developer communities are essential for building a loyal and enthusiastic user base.

Scalability remains a persistent challenge in the blockchain space, particularly for emerging cryptocurrencies aiming to compete with established networks. As user adoption grows, the network must be capable of handling increasing transaction volumes without sacrificing speed or security. Solving scalability challenges requires innovative consensus mechanisms, layer-two solutions, or sharding techniques that maintain decentralization while improving performance.

The inherent volatility of the cryptocurrency market presents a challenge for emerging cryptocurrencies seeking to establish stability and credibility. Extreme price fluctuations can deter potential investors and users who fear financial losses. Building investor confidence requires addressing market volatility and demonstrating the long-term viability of the project's technology, use cases, and community support.

Sourcing adequate funding and ensuring project sustainability is an ongoing challenge for emerging cryptocurrencies. While initial coin offerings (ICOs) and token sales were popular fundraising methods in the past, regulatory scrutiny and investor caution have led to more selective investment. Securing funding through partnerships, grants, venture capital, and other means is crucial for supporting ongoing development, marketing, and adoption efforts.

For emerging cryptocurrencies, maintaining a clear long-term strategy while adjusting to shifting market conditions and technology improvements is a delicate balancing act. Projects must remain agile and responsive to market trends, user feedback, and emerging challenges. Striking the right balance between staying true to the project's original vision and embracing necessary changes ensures continued relevance and growth.

Emerging cryptocurrencies are undoubtedly at the forefront of technological innovation and disruption within the cryptocurrency ecosystem. However, their journey is fraught with challenges that span market competition, technological development, regulatory compliance, security, adoption, and sustainability. Successfully navigating these challenges requires strategic planning, technical excellence, community engagement, regulatory awareness, and a commitment to a long-term vision. As the cryptocurrency landscape continues to evolve, emerging projects that can effectively address these challenges stand a better chance of leaving a lasting impact and contributing to the transformative potential of blockchain technology.

CHAPTER III

Technology Behind Emerging Cryptocurrencies

Smart contracts and their significance

Smart contracts, a foundational innovation in blockchain technology, have emerged as a pivotal driver of change within the cryptocurrency landscape. These self-executing contracts with predefined rules and conditions are encoded directly into code, enabling automation, transparency, and efficiency in various industries. As a crucial component of emerging cryptocurrencies, smart contracts have transformative potential that extends beyond traditional transactions. In this section, we delve into the significance of smart contracts as a technology behind emerging cryptocurrencies, exploring their capabilities, use cases, and impact on the evolving blockchain ecosystem.

Smart contracts streamline transactions and processes by automating their execution once predefined conditions are met. Due to the automation, traditional paper-based agreements no longer require middlemen, saving time and money. Smart contracts, for instance, can make property transfers easier in the real estate sector by immediately surrendering ownership rights if payment is confirmed. This efficiency expedites processes and minimizes the risk of human error and fraud.

Transparency is a fundamental principle of blockchain technology, and smart contracts contribute to this by providing transparent and tamper-proof execution of agreements. There will be no ambiguity or conflicts because all parties may see the contract's terms and conditions posted on the blockchain. This increased transparency fosters trust among parties, as the contract terms are immutable and accessible to all stakeholders.

Smart contracts can execute complex logic and conditions, creating intricate agreements that would be challenging to implement using traditional methods. Smart contracts, for instance, can be used in supply chain management to automatically pay suppliers once the goods have been received and verified, facilitating smooth communication between various parties. This capability expands the scope of use cases for blockchain technology beyond simple transactions.

Smart contracts are the foundation for decentralized applications (DApps) operating on blockchain platforms. These applications, from decentralized finance (DeFi) platforms to non-fungible token (NFT) marketplaces, rely on smart contracts to execute functions autonomously and securely. DApps allow for direct user-to-user communication without the use of middlemen by integrating business logic into smart contracts. The automation and efficiency offered by smart contracts can significantly reduce business operational costs. Traditional manual processes, especially those involving multiple intermediaries, are often time-consuming and resource-intensive. Automating these processes through smart contracts allows businesses to streamline their operations, lower costs, and allocate resources more effectively.

Smart contracts facilitate trustless transactions, where parties can transact without relying on a central authority or intermediary to enforce the terms. The code itself executes the contract, eliminating the need to trust a third party. This feature aligns with the core principles of blockchain technology, allowing for peer-to-peer transactions and interactions that do not require an intermediary.

Smart contracts can empower individuals lacking access to traditional financial services. Users can lend, borrow, and earn interest on their assets through DeFi platforms built on smart contracts without the help of a bank or other financial institution. This paves the way for greater financial inclusion and access to opportunities for individuals globally.

While smart contracts offer many benefits, they also face limitations and challenges. Coding errors or vulnerabilities in smart contracts can lead to security breaches or unintended outcomes. Additionally, smart contracts' legal recognition and enforcement vary across jurisdictions, raising questions about their legal validity. The complexity of some agreements may also make them challenging to encode accurately into code.

Smart contracts are a cornerstone technology that underpins the emergence of innovative cryptocurrencies and blockchain projects. Their significance lies in their ability to automate transactions, enhance transparency, facilitate complex logic, power decentralized applications, and reduce costs. By enabling trustless interactions and empowering financial inclusion, smart contracts drive the evolution of the blockchain ecosystem. As emerging cryptocurrencies continue to shape the future of finance, commerce, and various industries, smart contracts will remain a key enabler of their transformative potential, ushering in a new era of efficiency, transparency, and autonomy.

Consensus mechanisms: proof of work versus proof of stake versus others

Consensus mechanisms form the bedrock of blockchain technology, facilitating agreement and validation of transactions across decentralized networks. These mechanisms ensure that participants within a network reach a consensus on the state of the blockchain without relying on a central authority. Among the various consensus mechanisms, proof of work (PoW) and proof of stake (PoS) has emerged as the most prominent. However, the rapidly evolving landscape of emerging cryptocurrencies has given rise to other innovative consensus mechanisms. In this section, we explore the significance of consensus mechanisms as a technology behind emerging cryptocurrencies, focusing on the distinctions between PoW and PoS and exploring alternative consensus mechanisms.

Proof of work, introduced by Bitcoin's creator Satoshi Nakamoto, is the pioneering consensus mechanism. Miners compete against one another in proof-of-work (PoW) systems to solve difficult mathematical puzzles; the first miner to do so validates and adds a block of transactions to the blockchain. This energy-intensive process ensures the network's security, as altering a block would require immense computational power, making it economically infeasible for malicious actors to attack the network.

While PoW offers security, it comes with environmental concerns due to its energy consumption. The massive computational power required for mining contributes to carbon emissions and raises questions about the sustainability of the technology. PoW remains a stalwart choice for several established cryptocurrencies, including Bitcoin.

The energy efficiency issues with PoW are addressed by the alternative consensus mechanism known as proof of stake. In a proof-of-stake (PoS) system, validators are selected to add new blocks and approve transactions based on the quantity of cryptocurrencies they own and are willing to "stake" as security. Validators are encouraged to act honestly since they run the danger of losing their staked funds.

PoS uses less energy than PoW because it doesn't rely on computationally intensive processes. It also addresses the issue of centralization that can emerge in PoW networks due to the concentration of mining power in the hands of a few entities. However, PoS introduces new challenges, such as the "rich-get-richer" problem, where participants with more wealth have more influence over consensus decisions.

Delegated proof of stake is an evolution of PoS that introduces a layer of representative democracy into the consensus process. Token holders in DPoS elect a group of delegates who are in charge of approving transactions and constructing blocks. These delegates are typically rewarded with transaction fees or newly minted tokens. DPoS aims to achieve faster transaction confirmation times by limiting the number of validators and introducing a voting system that can be more efficient than traditional PoS. However, concerns about centralization arise, as the voting power of token holders may be concentrated among a few influential entities.

The consensus mechanism known as proof of authority depends on a chosen group of validators who have established identities and reputations. Validators are known entities, such as corporations or institutions, responsible for confirming transactions and maintaining the network's security.

PoA sacrifices decentralization for efficiency and security, as the validators are trusted entities with established reputations. While this mechanism reduces the risk of malicious behavior, it raises questions about the centralization of control and the potential for censorship.

Proof of space and time is a relatively new consensus mechanism that leverages unused storage space on participants' devices as collateral. This space is used to solve computational challenges, and the time taken to solve these challenges further reinforces the network's security.
PoST presents an energy-efficient alternative to PoW while utilizing existing resources. It is particularly appealing as a consensus mechanism for environmentally conscious projects that seek to minimize energy consumption.

Proof of capacity is a variant of PoST that utilizes participants' available disk space instead of computational power. Miners precompute solutions to computational puzzles and store them on their devices. The process of creating solutions is known as "plotting." When a new block needs validation, miners prove their precomputed solutions.

PoC addresses some of the concerns associated with PoW, such as high energy consumption and resource-intensive computations. It offers an environmentally friendly consensus mechanism that relies on storage capacity rather than computational power.

Consensus mechanisms represent the heart of blockchain technology, enabling the decentralized agreement and validation of transactions. Emerging cryptocurrencies are driven to explore alternative consensus mechanisms beyond the classic PoW and PoS to address energy consumption, centralization, scalability, and security concerns. While PoW offers security at the cost of energy efficiency, PoS focuses on energy-efficient solutions but may encounter centralization challenges. DPoS, PoA, PoST, and PoC present innovative alternatives that cater to various needs and priorities within the cryptocurrency ecosystem.

The choice of consensus mechanism is a pivotal decision that shapes the characteristics and goals of an emerging cryptocurrency. While each mechanism has advantages and challenges, they collectively contribute to the diversity and evolution of the blockchain landscape. Emerging cryptocurrencies will probably experiment and explore different consensus mechanisms as the technology develops, trying to find the ideal harmony between security, efficiency, decentralization, and scalability in the quest for a more inclusive and revolutionary blockchain future.

Interoperability and scalability solutions

The rapid evolution of the cryptocurrency landscape has given rise to a myriad of emerging cryptocurrencies, each vying to offer unique value propositions and solutions to address the limitations of existing platforms. Among the many challenges these new entrants face, interoperability and scalability stand out as crucial issues that demand innovative solutions. In this section, we delve into the significance of interoperability and scalability as technologies behind emerging cryptocurrencies, exploring their importance, the challenges they address, and the solutions that drive the advancement of the blockchain ecosystem.

Interoperability is the capacity of several blockchain networks to exchange information, conduct transactions, and communicate with one another without any problems. In the early days of blockchain technology, individual platforms operated as isolated silos, hindering the efficient flow of information and value between different networks. Interoperability addresses this challenge by enabling compatibility and interaction across diverse blockchains, regardless of their underlying protocols.

The widespread use of blockchain technology depends on interoperability. It opens up a new level of innovation and utility by enabling the development of decentralized applications (DApps) that take advantage of the benefits of various platforms. For example, a DApp could utilize the speed and scalability of one blockchain while benefiting from the security and consensus mechanisms of another. Emerging cryptocurrencies are increasingly focusing on interoperability solutions to foster collaboration, enhance user experiences, and maximize the potential of blockchain technology.

Scalability is a critical concern as blockchain networks strive to accommodate a growing number of users and transactions. The limited throughput of early blockchain platforms like Bitcoin and Ethereum led to congestion and high transaction fees during periods of high demand. Scalability solutions aim to address these bottlenecks by increasing the capacity of blockchain networks to process transactions and support DApps without compromising security or decentralization.

Emerging cryptocurrencies recognize that to achieve mass adoption and compete with traditional payment systems; they must offer seamless and fast transaction processing. Solutions such as sharding, layer-two protocols, and improved consensus mechanisms are employed to enhance the scalability of blockchain networks. These innovations pave the way for creating high-performance applications while maintaining the decentralization that is integral to the blockchain philosophy.

Layer-two solutions are a prominent approach to addressing scalability challenges. These solutions create an additional layer on top of the leading blockchain that handles many transactions off-chain, reducing the burden on the main network. Lightning Network for Bitcoin and the Polygon network for Ethereum are examples of layer-two solutions that enable faster and more cost-effective transactions.

Layer-two solutions offer the advantage of scalability without sacrificing the decentralization and security of the main blockchain. By offloading transactions to a secondary layer, layer-two solutions alleviate congestion and high fees, making blockchain networks more accessible and user-friendly. Emerging cryptocurrencies recognize the potential of layer-two solutions to enhance the performance of their platforms and attract users seeking efficiency and speed.

By splitting the network into smaller units, or "shards," capable of carrying out transactions on their own, the sharding technique aims to increase the scalability of blockchains. Blockchain networks can significantly increase their transaction throughput and capacity by distributing the workload among multiple shards.

Emerging cryptocurrencies leverage sharding to enhance their scalability while maintaining a decentralized structure. Ethereum, for instance, is actively working on Ethereum 2.0, a major upgrade that introduces sharding to the network. Sharding offers a promising solution to the scalability challenge by allowing blockchain platforms to process transactions in parallel and accommodate the growing demands of a global user base.
Cross-chain bridges facilitate interoperability by creating connections between different blockchain networks. These bridges enable assets and data to move seamlessly between blockchains, unlocking new possibilities for cross-chain applications and value transfers.

Emerging cryptocurrencies recognize that cross-chain bridges are essential for fostering collaboration and expanding the utility of their platforms. By enabling assets to flow freely across multiple blockchains, cross-chain bridges enhance the interoperability of emerging cryptocurrencies and contribute to the growth of a more interconnected and collaborative blockchain ecosystem.

Projects like Polkadot have emerged as dedicated platforms for addressing interoperability and scalability challenges. With Polkadot, many blockchains may be linked together into a single network and share information and transactions while still keeping their individual security and consensus mechanisms. Polkadot's approach demonstrates the growing recognition of the importance of interoperability and scalability in cryptocurrency. Its architecture facilitates interoperability and enables the parallel processing of transactions through its relay chain and parachains, offering a scalable solution for emerging cryptocurrencies seeking to enhance their performance.

Interoperability and scalability are pivotal technologies shaping the development and success of emerging cryptocurrencies. Interoperability bridges the gap between isolated blockchain networks, enabling collaboration, innovation, and a more connected ecosystem. Scalability solutions address the challenge of processing a higher volume of transactions, enhancing blockchain platforms' usability and competitiveness. Emerging cryptocurrencies recognize that addressing interoperability and scalability challenges is essential for gaining adoption and realizing the transformative potential of blockchain technology. Through layer-two solutions, sharding techniques, cross-chain bridges, and dedicated platforms like Polkadot, these cryptocurrencies are advancing the technological frontier, building bridges between networks, and creating solutions that can support the demands of a global and interconnected world. As the blockchain landscape continues to evolve, the significance of interoperability and scalability as technologies behind emerging cryptocurrencies will remain central to shaping the future of decentralized finance, commerce, and digital innovation.

Innovation in blockchain technology within the emerging cryptocurrency space

The emerging cryptocurrency market is a hive of invention that is continually pushing the limits of what is feasible with blockchain technology. As new projects emerge and seek to differentiate themselves, they bring a wave of creative solutions, novel use cases, and groundbreaking features that redefine the landscape. In this section, we delve into the innovation that drives blockchain technology within the emerging cryptocurrency space, exploring the key areas of advancement, the impact on numerous industries, and the transformative potential of these innovations.

Decentralized finance (DeFi) is one of the most transformative and innovative developments in the emerging cryptocurrency space. The creation of decentralized and permissionless versions of standard financial services is the goal of projects known as DeFi. These projects make use of blockchain technology and cover various financial services, including lending, borrowing, trading, insurance, and yield farming.

DeFi is revolutionary because it eliminates intermediaries, reduces costs, and increases accessibility to financial services for individuals worldwide. Protocols like Compound, Aave, and MakerDAO enable users to lend their assets and earn interest, borrow against their holdings, and generate yield by providing liquidity to decentralized exchanges. The innovation in DeFi extends to algorithmic stablecoins, which maintain their value through smart contracts and algorithmic mechanisms rather than being backed by traditional assets.

Non-fungible tokens (NFTs) have captured the world's attention as a remarkable innovation within the blockchain space. On a blockchain, non-fungible tokens (NFTs) are used to represent one-of-a-kind digital assets such as works of art, music, collectibles, and virtual real estate. Unlike cryptocurrencies, NFTs cannot be exchanged on a one-to-one basis due to their distinct characteristics.

NFTs have unlocked new opportunities for artists, creators, and collectors to tokenize and trade digital assets, providing a new revenue stream and enabling verifiable ownership in the digital realm. Innovations in NFTs extend to metaverse projects that envision virtual worlds where ownership of digital assets, land, and experiences is secured through blockchain technology. This innovation could reshape the entertainment, gaming, and creative industries.

Interoperability solutions have emerged as a response to the fragmentation and isolation of different blockchain networks. These solutions aim to enable seamless communication and value transfer between other blockchains. Projects like Polkadot, Cosmos, and Avalanche introduce cross-chain protocols that facilitate interoperability, enabling assets and data to move freely across diverse blockchain ecosystems.

Cross-chain interoperability opens up a new realm of possibilities by allowing different blockchains to collaborate and share resources. This innovation enhances the utility of cryptocurrencies, enables efficient asset transfers, and fosters collaboration among diverse projects, ultimately contributing to a more interconnected and efficient blockchain ecosystem.

As blockchain networks grow in popularity, the scalability challenge becomes more pronounced. Layer-two scaling solutions address this challenge by creating a further layer on top of the main blockchain, where transactions can be processed more efficiently and at a lower cost.

Innovations like the Lightning Network for Bitcoin and the Polygon network for Ethereum utilize layer-two solutions to increase transaction throughput while maintaining the security and decentralization of the underlying blockchain. These solutions allow blockchain networks to handle larger transactions without compromising user experience or straining network resources.

Privacy and security are paramount in cryptocurrency, and emerging projects are driving innovation in this arena. Privacy-focused cryptocurrencies like Monero and Zcash utilize advanced cryptographic techniques to enhance users' anonymity. These cryptocurrencies enable private transactions, shielding the sender, recipient, and transaction amount from prying eyes.

Moreover, innovations in zero-knowledge proofs and secure multi-party computation have paved the way for privacy-preserving smart contracts. These advancements allow for the execution of complex computations without revealing sensitive data, opening up new possibilities for healthcare, finance, and identity verification applications. Environmental sustainability is a pressing concern in blockchain, mainly due to the energy-intensive nature of proof-of-work (PoW) consensus mechanisms. Emerging projects are seeking innovative alternatives, such as proof-of-stake (PoS), delegated proof-of-stake (DPoS), and proof-of-space (PoSpace), which consume significantly less energy while still maintaining the integrity of the blockchain.

Ethereum's transition to Ethereum 2.0, which introduces a PoS consensus mechanism, is a notable example of innovation driven by sustainability concerns. These innovations reduce the carbon footprint associated with blockchain operations and position emerging cryptocurrencies as more environmentally responsible alternatives.

Decentralized autonomous organizations (DAOs) represent a paradigm shift in governance and decision-making within the cryptocurrency space. DAOs operate through smart contracts, enabling participants to collectively make decisions, allocate resources, and manage projects without the need for a centralized authority.

DAOs empower community members to play an active role in shaping the direction of cryptocurrency projects. Proposals, voting mechanisms, and transparent decision-making processes create a more democratic and inclusive approach to project governance. DAOs are being adopted by emerging cryptocurrencies to enhance community engagement, transparency, and the decentralized nature of their platforms.

Innovation within the emerging cryptocurrency space drives transformative changes that extend beyond finance. From DeFi's disruption of traditional financial services to NFTs' tokenization of digital assets, and from cross-chain interoperability's bridging of blockchain networks to privacy-enhancing technologies' protection of user data, these innovations are reshaping industries and expanding the potential of blockchain technology.

The spirit of innovation that characterizes the emerging cryptocurrency space is not only about technological advancement but also about challenging existing paradigms and envisioning new possibilities. These technologies, as they continue to develop and mature, have the potential to completely alter the financial landscape as well as the ways in which we communicate with one another, create, and do business in the digital age. The world watches as the emerging cryptocurrency space paves the way for a more decentralized, efficient, and interconnected future.

CHAPTER IV

Investment Strategies for Altcoins

Risk assessment and risk management in altcoin investments

Altcoins, or alternative cryptocurrencies, have gained significant attention and popularity in the ever-evolving landscape of digital assets. Although Bitcoin is still the most well-known cryptocurrency, alternative coins provide investors with the potential to diversify their holdings and earn considerable returns. However, the world of altcoin investments has risks. As the market expands, understanding and effectively managing these risks become paramount. In this section, we delve into the intricacies of risk assessment and risk management in altcoin investments, exploring the various risks associated with these assets and the strategies investors can employ to navigate this dynamic landscape.

One of the most prominent characteristics of the cryptocurrency market, including altcoins, is its inherent volatility. While volatility can lead to significant gains, it can also result in substantial losses. Altcoin prices can experience extreme fluctuations within short periods, driven by market sentiment, regulatory developments, technological advancements, and macroeconomic trends. Investors must be prepared for the possibility of sharp price declines and rapid price surges.

The cryptocurrency market, including altcoins, operates within a regulatory environment that varies across jurisdictions. Some altcoins may fall into regulatory grey areas, leading to uncertainty about their legal status and potential future regulatory changes. Additionally, the lack of investor protection mechanisms common in traditional financial markets can expose investors to risks, such as scams, fraud, and market manipulation. It is essential, in order to effectively manage these risks, to carry out exhaustive due diligence investigations and to keep oneself updated with new regulatory requirements.

Altcoins often introduce new technologies and concepts that can carry technical risks. Smart contract vulnerabilities, bugs in the underlying blockchain code, and security breaches can lead to the loss of funds and damage to the project's reputation. Investors should evaluate the project's technical documentation, development team, security audits, and response to past vulnerabilities to assess the level of technical risk associated with an altcoin.

The ease with which an asset can be bought or sold without causing a major change in its price is referred to as its liquidity. Many altcoins, especially those with smaller market capitalizations, may have lower liquidity than established cryptocurrencies like Bitcoin and Ethereum. This lack of liquidity can make entering or exiting positions at desired prices challenging, potentially leading to slippage and higher trading costs. Investors should consider liquidity when evaluating altcoin investments and be prepared for potential trading challenges.

Altcoin markets, especially those with lower trading volumes, can be susceptible to market manipulation and pump-and-dump schemes. In a pump-and-dump, the price of an altcoin is artificially inflated through coordinated buying, followed by a sudden sell-off that leaves unsuspecting investors with losses. It is essential to be cautious of projects with sudden and unexplained price spikes, as they could indicate manipulative activities.

A comprehensive understanding of the fundamentals of the project as well as the use cases is required prior to investing in alternative coins. Some altcoins may lack a clear value proposition, utility, or real-world application, negatively impacting their long-term viability. Investors should assess whether the altcoin addresses a genuine problem, has a competitive advantage, and has a clear roadmap for development and adoption.

The white paper is a fundamental document that outlines an altcoin's goals, technology, and vision. However, not all projects deliver on the promises made in their white papers. Some projects may overstate their capabilities or make unrealistic claims to attract investors. The feasibility of the project's aims, technology, and timing should be thoroughly evaluated by investors, and they should also analyze whether the team has an established history of delivering on their commitments.

Diversification is a fundamental principle of risk management in any investment portfolio, including altcoins. Spreading investments across different altcoins can help mitigate the impact of poor performance from a single asset. However, diversification should be balanced with thorough research and due diligence, as blindly investing in a wide range of altcoins without understanding their fundamentals can expose investors to unnecessary risks.

The cryptocurrency market is dynamic and rapidly evolving. Staying informed about market trends, technological advancements, regulatory changes, and project developments is crucial for managing risks effectively. Continuous research guarantees that investors are aware of the most recent information and can make judgments that are educated based on the conditions of the market at the time.

Altcoin investments should align with investors' risk tolerance and long-term financial goals. The cryptocurrency market is known for its cycles of price volatility, and short-term price fluctuations are common. A focus on the long term can assist investors in weathering market downturns and positioning themselves to profit from potential future growth.

Altcoin investments offer a world of opportunity and innovation, but they also come with their fair share of risks. To navigate this dynamic landscape successfully, investors must engage in rigorous risk assessment and employ adequate risk management strategies. By understanding the risks associated with altcoins, conducting thorough due diligence, diversifying their portfolios, staying informed, and maintaining a long-term perspective, investors can capitalize on the potential rewards while mitigating the inherent uncertainties of the emerging cryptocurrency space.

Fundamental analysis of emerging cryptocurrencies

As the cryptocurrency landscape continues to evolve, emerging cryptocurrencies are capturing the attention of investors seeking to diversify their portfolios and capitalize on innovative technologies. Fundamental analysis is a critical tool for evaluating these new digital assets' potential value and viability. While price volatility remains a characteristic of the cryptocurrency market, the fundamental analysis provides investors with a systematic approach to assessing the underlying factors that drive an emerging cryptocurrency's growth and adoption. In this section, we delve into the intricacies of fundamental analysis for emerging cryptocurrencies, exploring the key components, methodologies, and considerations that guide investors in making informed decisions within this dynamic and evolving space.

In fundamental analysis, an asset's "intrinsic value" is evaluated by analyzing its underlying factors, such as its technology, use case, adoption, team, market trends, and competitive landscape. This is done in order to determine the "true" value of the asset. This approach determines whether an asset is overvalued or undervalued based on its fundamental strengths and weaknesses. In emerging cryptocurrencies, fundamental analysis provides insights into these digital assets' potential long-term viability and growth prospects.

At the core of any emerging cryptocurrency is its underlying technology. Investors should assess the innovation and uniqueness of the technology, including its consensus mechanism, scalability solutions, privacy features, interoperability, and security protocols. A robust technological foundation can differentiate an emerging cryptocurrency and position it as a frontrunner in its niche.

Fundamental analysis involves evaluating an emerging cryptocurrency's utility and real-world use cases. A project with a clear and practical use case that addresses a genuine problem in a specific industry or sector will likely gain adoption and value over time. Investors should assess the project's value proposition and its potential to disrupt existing systems or create new economic models.

The development team behind an emerging cryptocurrency plays a pivotal role in its success. Investors should scrutinize the team's experience, expertise, and track record in fields such as blockchain technology, cryptography, finance, and software development. Transparent communication, a strong vision, and a history of delivering on commitments are indicators of a capable and dedicated team.

A thriving and engaged community is a positive indicator of an emerging cryptocurrency's potential. Community engagement, partnerships, and collaborations can contribute to increased adoption, network effects, and the project's growth. Investors should assess the project's social media presence, active community discussions, and partnerships with industry players.

Evaluating market trends and the competitive landscape is crucial for understanding an emerging cryptocurrency's potential challenges and opportunities. Investors should analyze how the project differentiates itself from existing competitors and how it positions itself to capitalize on emerging trends within the broader cryptocurrency ecosystem.

The regulatory environment can significantly impact the success and adoption of an emerging cryptocurrency. Investors should consider the project's compliance with relevant regulations, data privacy approach, and legal status in different jurisdictions. Projects that proactively address regulatory challenges are more likely to navigate the complexities of the legal landscape successfully.

Tokenomics is the economic model of a cryptocurrency, including factors such as token supply, distribution, inflation rate, and mechanisms for incentivizing network participants. Investors should assess whether the tokenomics align with the project's goals, contribute to a healthy ecosystem, and provide incentives for long-term participation.

Fundamental analysis also involves identifying and evaluating potential risks of an emerging cryptocurrency. These risks can range from technological vulnerabilities and regulatory uncertainties to market adoption challenges and competition from other projects. Investors should conduct a thorough risk assessment and consider how each risk factor could impact the project's long-term prospects.

Ultimately, the fundamental analysis aims to determine an emerging cryptocurrency's long-term viability and growth potential. By carefully evaluating the project's technology, use cases, team, adoption, market trends, regulatory compliance, and risk factors, investors can comprehensively understand the project's strengths and weaknesses.

Fundamental analysis serves as a guiding compass for investors navigating the world of emerging cryptocurrencies. While the cryptocurrency market remains inherently volatile, a solid foundation of fundamental analysis equips investors with the tools to make informed decisions. By evaluating technology, utility, team, adoption, market trends, regulatory considerations, and risk factors, investors can assess an emerging cryptocurrency's potential value and viability. In a landscape characterized by innovation and change, the fundamental analysis provides a systematic approach to identifying projects with the potential to shape the future of finance, technology, and industries worldwide.

Technical analysis and chart patterns for altcoin trading

Altcoin trading within the cryptocurrency market is characterized by its dynamic and rapidly changing nature. While fundamental analysis provides insights into the underlying factors that drive the value of emerging cryptocurrencies, technical analysis offers traders a valuable toolkit for understanding price movements and making informed trading decisions. For the purpose of forecasting future price movements, technical analysis entails looking at previous price data, chart patterns, and indicators. In this section, we delve into the intricacies of technical analysis and chart patterns for altcoin trading, exploring how these tools can be utilized to identify trends, points of entry and exit, and potential opportunities within the volatile world of altcoin trading.

The foundation of technical analysis is the idea that past price and volume data can provide useful insights into the direction that prices are likely to move in the future. By analyzing patterns, trends, and indicators, traders seek to anticipate market sentiment and identify potential supply and demand dynamics shifts. While fundamental analysis delves into the intrinsic value of an asset, technical analysis focuses on patterns and trends that can indicate price direction.

Traders utilize chart patterns, which are visual representations of past market movements, to forecast price trends. These patterns are formed by the interplay of supply and demand forces and can provide valuable insights into market sentiment. Some common chart patterns include:

Head and Shoulders: Three peaks make up this pattern, with the middle peak (the head) standing higher compared to the other two (shoulders). It often indicates a trend reversal from bullish to bearish.

Double Top/Bottom: These patterns consist of two peaks or troughs, indicating a potential reversal of the prevailing trend.

Ascending/Descending Triangles: Triangles formed by converging trendlines suggest a potential breakout in the direction of the prevailing trend.

Cup and Handle: This pattern resembles a teacup and a handle and is often seen as a bullish continuation pattern.

Flag and Pennant: These patterns are characterized by a sharp price movement (flagpole) followed by a consolidation (flag or pennant), typically indicating a continuation of the trend.

Moving averages are widely used indicators that help traders identify trends and smooth out short-term price fluctuations. Simple moving averages (SMA) and exponential moving averages (EMA) are commonly used to analyze price data over specific periods. Long-term and short-term moving averages intersecting might indicate probable trend reversals or continuations.

A momentum oscillator called Relative Strength Index (RSI) gauges the rapidity and variety of price changes. It measures overbought and oversold circumstances and spans from 0 to 100. An asset may be overbought and due for a downturn if the RSI reading is above 70, while an asset may be oversold and due for a potential rebound if the RSI reading is below 30.

Based on the Fibonacci sequence, Fibonacci retracement levels can be used to pinpoint probable levels of support and resistance. Traders often use these levels to identify areas where an asset's price might experience a pullback or reversal.

A thorough indicator, the Ichimoku Cloud sheds light on trends, levels of support and resistance, and probable entry and exit locations. It consists of five lines, including the cloud (Kumo), and can be a valuable tool for traders looking for a holistic view of an asset's price dynamics.

When applying technical analysis to altcoin trading, traders must consider the unique characteristics of the cryptocurrency market. Cryptocurrencies are known for their high volatility, rapid price movements, and susceptibility to market sentiment. As a result, technical analysis can provide valuable insights into short-term trends and potential entry and exit points.

While technical analysis offers valuable tools for altcoin trading, it's essential to approach it with caution and a solid understanding of its limitations. The cryptocurrency market can be influenced by external factors, news events, and regulatory developments that may not be reflected in historical price data. Additionally, traders need to be mindful of possible market manipulation and how low liquidity affects price changes.

Effective altcoin trading often involves an integration of both technical and fundamental analysis. While technical analysis provides insights into price movements and trends, fundamental analysis helps traders understand an altcoin's underlying value proposition, adoption potential, and competitive landscape. By combining these approaches, traders can make more informed and well-rounded trading decisions.

Technical analysis and chart patterns play a crucial role in altcoin trading by giving traders insights into price movements, trends, and potential entry and exit points. As the cryptocurrency market evolves, these tools offer valuable insights to help traders navigate the dynamic landscape of altcoin trading. However, it's essential to approach technical analysis with a clear understanding of its strengths and limitations, considering external factors that can impact price movements. By integrating technical analysis with fundamental analysis and staying informed about market developments, traders can enhance their ability to make informed decisions and capitalize on opportunities within the volatile and exciting world of altcoin trading.

Diversification and portfolio management

Altcoin trading, within the dynamic and often unpredictable cryptocurrency market, offers investors opportunities for significant gains but also exposes them to heightened risks. Diversification and effective portfolio management are essential strategies for navigating this volatile landscape, where emerging cryptocurrencies can experience rapid price fluctuations and unexpected shifts in market sentiment. In this section, we explore the significance of diversification and portfolio management for altcoin trading, examining their benefits, best practices, and how these strategies can enhance risk mitigation and potential returns in the ever-evolving world of digital assets.

Investing is predicated on a number of fundamental principles, one of which is diversification, which is the practice of spreading one's investments over a variety of assets in order to lower overall risk. In the context of altcoin trading, diversification goes beyond merely holding multiple cryptocurrencies; it involves selecting assets with low correlation. By diversifying a portfolio, investors aim to limit exposure to the potential downfall of any single asset while increasing the potential for gains through the performance of other assets.

The cryptocurrency market is notorious for being extremely volatile, which may lead to either significant gains or significant losses. Diversification helps mitigate the impact of extreme price fluctuations. When one asset experiences a significant decline, others in the portfolio may not be affected similarly. This cushioning effect can help investors weather downturns and avoid catastrophic losses.

Diversification in altcoin trading involves selecting a mix of altcoins representing different sectors, technologies, and use cases. Each altcoin should have its unique value proposition, reducing the risk associated with a single project's failure or underperformance. A diversified portfolio might entail a combination of decentralized finance (DeFi) tokens, privacy-focused coins, smart contract platforms, and assets with utility in emerging sectors like gaming or metaverse.

Diversification allows investors to strike a balance between risk and potential reward. While some altcoins might offer higher returns due to their riskier nature, others may provide stability and security. By diversifying their investments, traders can participate in the growth potential of high-risk, high-reward assets while also maintaining exposure to more stable assets.

Rebalancing is a strategy that entails making periodic changes to the distribution of assets within a portfolio in order to keep the portfolio's risk and reward profile in line with the investor's preferences. As the cryptocurrency market evolves and altcoins' performance varies, the initial allocation of assets may shift. Rebalancing ensures that the portfolio remains aligned with the investor's goals and risk tolerance.

Concentration risk refers to the potential loss that can arise from holding a disproportionately large amount of a single asset. This risk is particularly relevant in the altcoin market, where projects can experience extreme price fluctuations. Diversification helps mitigate concentration risk by spreading investments across multiple assets, minimizing the impact of a single asset's poor performance on the overall portfolio.
Understanding the correlation between different altcoins is crucial for effective diversification. Low or negative correlation means that the price movements of two assets are less likely to occur simultaneously. The high correlation suggests that the assets' prices move similarly. Investors should include assets with varying degrees of correlation to achieve a well-diversified portfolio.
While diversification is essential, it's possible to over-diversify a portfolio to the point where it becomes challenging to manage effectively. Holding too many assets can dilute potential gains and make monitoring individual assets' performance and news difficult. It is essential to find the right balance between having a diversified portfolio and being able to easily manage it.

Effective portfolio management requires ongoing monitoring of market developments, news, and trends.

The cryptocurrency market is highly dynamic, and projects can experience rapid shifts in sentiment and fundamentals. Staying informed helps investors make timely decisions regarding rebalancing, adjustments, and potential additions or removals from the portfolio.

Effective portfolio management involves integrating both fundamental and technical analysis. While diversification is based on fundamental factors such as the technology, use case, and team behind each altcoin, technical analysis provides insights into price movements, trends, and potential entry and exit points. Combining these approaches enhances the ability to make informed decisions about the portfolio's composition.
Successful portfolio management requires discipline and patience. The cryptocurrency market can be emotionally charged, with rapid price movements causing FOMO (fear of missing out) and panic selling. Sticking to a well-thought-out diversification strategy and avoiding impulsive decisions are essential for long-term success. The altcoin market constantly evolves, with new projects, technologies, and trends emerging regularly. Portfolio management should be adaptable to accommodate changes in the market landscape. This includes staying open to re-evaluating the portfolio's composition and considering new opportunities as they arise.
Diversification and portfolio management are indispensable strategies for navigating the complex and volatile landscape of altcoin trading. Investors can reduce risk, increase possible returns, and position themselves to benefit from the dynamic character of the cryptocurrency market by spreading their investments over a variety of assets with different risk profiles, correlations, and technology. Effective portfolio

management involves carefully balancing diversification, periodic rebalancing, and a deep understanding of each asset's fundamentals and technical trends. In a world where innovation and uncertainty coexist, mastering these strategies is essential for achieving success and longevity in altcoin trading.

CHAPTER V

Regulatory Landscape and Legal Considerations

Global regulatory trends for cryptocurrencies and altcoins

The rise of cryptocurrencies and altcoins has ushered in a new era of digital finance, presenting unprecedented opportunities and challenges for economies worldwide. As the value of these digital assets continues to rise, governments and regulatory organizations all over the world are struggling to come up with a legal framework that balances protecting investors, fostering innovation, and maintaining financial stability. In this section, we delve into the intricate landscape of global regulatory trends for cryptocurrencies and altcoins, exploring the
diverse approaches taken by different countries, the challenges of harmonizing regulations across borders, and the potential impact of evolving regulatory environments on the future of digital finance.

Regulatory attitudes toward cryptocurrencies and altcoins span a broad spectrum, ranging from open embrace to outright prohibition. Some countries have embraced these digital assets, recognizing their potential for economic growth, innovation, and financial inclusion. Others remain cautious due to concerns about consumer protection, money laundering, tax evasion, and their potential impact on traditional financial systems.

The United States and Canada have adopted diverse regulatory approaches in North America. The U.S. has seen a complex interplay of federal and state regulations, with different agencies having varying interpretations of cryptocurrencies. Regulatory bodies like the SEC have focused on determining whether specific cryptocurrencies are securities, while other initiatives aim to enhance consumer protection. Conversely, Canada has adopted a more proactive approach, developing a regulatory sandbox to encourage innovation while ensuring investor protection.

Europe showcases a patchwork of regulatory approaches as well. While countries like Switzerland and Malta have positioned themselves as crypto-friendly jurisdictions, the European Union has been developing a thorough regulatory framework to handle the issues with cryptocurrencies and alternative coins. The EU's proposed MiCA (Markets in Crypto-Assets) regulation seeks to establish a harmonized blockchain framework, providing legal clarity while fostering innovation and consumer protection.

Asian countries have displayed a range of regulatory stances. Japan, for example, introduced a licensing framework for cryptocurrency exchanges and recognized Bitcoin as a legal tender. In contrast, China has taken a more stringent approach, imposing bans on various aspects of cryptocurrency trading and ICOs (Initial Coin Offerings). While initially displaying caution, India has shown signs of reevaluating its stance, aiming to balance innovation with concerns about consumer protection and financial stability.

A central challenge for regulators is balancing fostering innovation and safeguarding investors and financial systems. Cryptocurrencies and altcoins offer groundbreaking opportunities, including decentralized finance (DeFi), non-fungible tokens (NFTs), and smart contracts. However, the absence of traditional intermediaries and the pseudonymous nature of transactions raise concerns about fraud, market manipulation, and inadequate investor recourse.

Cryptocurrencies' potential for anonymity and borderless transactions has raised concerns about their misuse for money laundering, terrorist financing, and other illicit activities. Regulatory trends include implementing Anti-Money Laundering (AML) and Know Your Customer (KYC) requirements for cryptocurrency exchanges and wallet providers. Striking a balance between privacy and compliance remains a challenge, as robust AML measures can impact the privacy-enhancing features of specific cryptocurrencies.

The taxation of cryptocurrencies has been a topic of ongoing debate. Different countries have taken varied approaches, treating cryptocurrencies as property, commodities, or even currency. The lack of standardized taxation rules for cryptocurrencies and altcoins can confuse users and impose reporting burdens on individuals and businesses.

To foster innovation while maintaining oversight, some jurisdictions have introduced regulatory sandboxes. Under regulatory supervision, these frameworks allow businesses to experiment with new technologies and business models. Sandboxes enable startups to develop and test their ideas while collaborating with regulators to ensure compliance and consumer protection.

Cryptocurrencies' decentralized and borderless nature poses challenges for regulators attempting to enforce national regulations. Cryptocurrency transactions can occur across international boundaries, making tracking and regulating activities difficult. This challenge has spurred discussions about international cooperation and the need for harmonized regulatory frameworks to address cross-border transactions and challenges.

Clear and transparent regulations are essential for fostering investor confidence and encouraging participation in the cryptocurrency market. Regulatory uncertainty can lead to hesitation among institutional investors, potentially stifling the growth and maturity of the market. The risk of regulatory violations is decreased by the regulations' clarity, which helps market players understand their rights and responsibilities.

Without uniform global regulations, self-regulatory initiatives and industry standards have emerged to establish best practices and guidelines. Organizations such as the Blockchain Association and the Crypto Rating Council aim to clarify how existing regulations apply to cryptocurrencies. These initiatives can help bridge the gap between technological innovation and regulatory compliance.

As the cryptocurrency market evolves, so will its regulatory landscape. Governments and regulators will likely adapt their approaches based on the development of new technologies, market trends, and feedback from stakeholders. The increasing involvement of institutional investors, advancements in decentralized technologies, and the market's maturation will all play a role in shaping the future regulatory environment.

The global regulatory trends for cryptocurrencies and altcoins are characterized by diversity, complexity, and ongoing evolution. As governments grapple with the challenges and opportunities presented by these digital assets, the need for a balanced approach that fosters innovation while ensuring investor protection becomes paramount. The harmonization of regulations across borders, the development of industry standards, and the engagement of stakeholders are essential factors in shaping a regulatory environment that fosters responsible growth, innovation, and long-term sustainability in digital finance.

Legal challenges and uncertainties in the altcoin market

The altcoin market, characterized by its innovation and potential for disruption, exists in a legal gray area that presents a multitude of challenges and uncertainties. As emerging cryptocurrencies and digital assets gain traction, governments, regulatory bodies, and legal experts are grappling with the complex task of applying existing legal frameworks to this rapidly evolving landscape. In this section, we delve into the intricate legal challenges and uncertainties faced by the altcoin market, exploring issues such as regulatory ambiguity, classification dilemmas, cross-border complexities, investor protection, and the potential for future legal developments that could shape the trajectory of the digital finance ecosystem.

The dynamic and borderless nature of cryptocurrencies poses significant challenges for regulators seeking to enforce existing laws in this new context. Regulatory ambiguity arises from the lack of clear definitions and classifications for cryptocurrencies and altcoins. The question of whether they should be treated as commodities, securities, currencies, or entirely new asset classes remains unanswered in many jurisdictions. This ambiguity can hinder innovation, create compliance difficulties for businesses, and impact investor confidence.

Determining whether a particular altcoin qualifies as a security is a critical legal challenge. Securities and Exchange Commission of the United States uses the "Howey Test" to assess whether an investment contract constitutes a security. However, applying this test to altcoins, which often have unique characteristics like utility tokens, can be complex. The classification of an altcoin as a security can subject its issuer to stringent regulatory requirements, impacting fundraising efforts and business operations.

The global nature of the altcoin market raises challenges related to jurisdiction and cross-border transactions. Cryptocurrency transactions can occur without regard for geographic boundaries, making it difficult for regulatory bodies to apply national laws effectively. The absence of a harmonized international regulatory framework creates challenges for enforcement, compliance, and addressing fraudulent or illicit activities that span multiple jurisdictions.

Anti-Money Laundering (or AML) and Know Your Customer (or KYC) regulations seek to prevent illegal activities such as money laundering and terrorist financing. However, the pseudonymous nature of many altcoins presents challenges for implementing robust AML and KYC procedures without compromising users' privacy. Striking a balance between regulatory compliance and users' privacy rights remains an ongoing challenge.

Smart contracts, a fundamental feature of many altcoin platforms, pose unique legal challenges. While smart contracts can automate and facilitate transactions, their self-executing nature can create complications in cases of disputes, errors, or unforeseen circumstances. Determining legal recourse and responsibility when issues arise from smart contract execution remains uncharted territory.

The altcoin market is susceptible to scams, fraud, and market manipulation due to its lack of traditional investor protections. Pump-and-dump schemes, fake initial coin offerings (ICOs), and deceptive marketing practices have victimized unsuspecting investors. The absence of comprehensive regulations can expose investors to significant risks and deter institutional participation.

The taxation of altcoins presents intricate challenges, as the unique characteristics of these assets often defy traditional tax classifications. Different jurisdictions may treat altcoins as property, commodities, or even currency, leading to confusion for investors and complicating tax reporting and compliance.

The legal challenges and uncertainties in the altcoin market are likely to drive future legal developments aimed at providing clarity and investor protection. Governments and regulatory bodies are under increasing pressure to adapt to the changing landscape. Potential developments include the introduction of new regulations specific to cryptocurrencies, the establishment of clearer definitions for different types of altcoins, and international collaboration to address cross-border challenges.

In the absence of comprehensive regulations, industry initiatives and self-regulation play a crucial role in shaping responsible practices within the altcoin market. Organizations like the Crypto Rating Council and the Blockchain Association aim to provide clarity on how existing regulations apply to different altcoins. These initiatives can bridge the gap between technological innovation and regulatory compliance.

Given the legal complexities of the altcoin market, participants should adopt a proactive approach to compliance and risk management. Conducting thorough due diligence, staying informed about regulatory developments, implementing robust AML and KYC procedures, and seeking legal counsel are critical steps for businesses and investors.

The altcoin market's legal challenges and uncertainties underscore the need for a balanced and adaptable regulatory approach that fosters innovation while safeguarding investors and financial systems. As governments, regulatory bodies, and legal experts grapple with the complexities of this evolving landscape, the potential for future legal developments and industry-driven standards could provide much-needed clarity and investor protection. The ongoing dialogue between the altcoin ecosystem and regulatory authorities will shape the trajectory of the digital finance revolution, guiding the industry toward responsible growth, innovation, and long-term sustainability.

Compliance and best practices for altcoin projects

As the altcoin market continues to expand and gain traction, altcoin projects are faced with a unique set of challenges related to regulatory compliance, investor protection, and responsible innovation. Navigating the evolving landscape of cryptocurrency regulations and ensuring adherence to best practices is crucial for building trust, attracting investment, and driving sustainable growth. In this section, we explore the importance of compliance and best practices for altcoin projects, examining key considerations such as regulatory frameworks, transparency, security, community engagement, and the role of self-regulation in fostering a responsible and thriving altcoin ecosystem.

The regulatory landscape for altcoin projects varies significantly across jurisdictions, from proactive approaches that encourage innovation to cautious regulatory environments concerned with investor protection. Altcoin projects must understand the legal requirements and obligations that apply to them within their operating jurisdictions. This includes complying with securities laws, anti-money laundering (AML) and know your customer (KYC) regulations, tax obligations, and consumer protection laws.

Rather than viewing regulatory compliance as a hindrance, altcoin projects can leverage it as a competitive advantage. Compliant projects are more likely to attract institutional investors, partnerships, and users who prioritize security and legitimacy. Compliance can also foster trust within the community and contribute to a positive reputation in the broader cryptocurrency ecosystem.

Transparency is paramount in the altcoin space. Projects should provide clear and accurate information about their technology, use case, team members, token distribution, fundraising methods, and future plans. Regularly updated whitepapers, roadmaps, and financial disclosures can demonstrate the project's commitment to openness and accountability.

Security breaches, hacks, and vulnerabilities can severely damage an altcoin project's reputation and value. Implementing robust security measures, conducting third-party security audits, and regularly updating and patching vulnerabilities are essential steps to mitigate risks and protect both the project and its community.

Engaging with the project's community is essential for building a strong user base and fostering a sense of ownership. Altcoin projects should establish clear communication channels, provide regular updates, and actively engage in discussions. Additionally, projects that involve the community in decision-making processes through decentralized governance mechanisms can enhance decentralization and inclusivity.

The way altcoin projects distribute their tokens can significantly impact community trust and adoption. Fair and ethical token distribution practices, such as avoiding pre-mining or pre-allocation to insiders, can promote a more equitable and decentralized ecosystem.

Projects seeking to conduct initial coin offerings (ICOs) or token sales should prioritize investor protection. This includes providing potential investors with comprehensive information about the project, its technology, and its financials. Investors should conduct thorough due diligence before participating in any altcoin project to understand the risks and potential returns.

In the absence of comprehensive regulations, altcoin projects can take the initiative to self-regulate and adopt industry standards. Organizations like the Crypto Rating Council and the Blockchain Association provide frameworks for evaluating the potential regulatory implications of altcoins. Self-regulation can help projects align with best practices and enhance transparency.

Altcoin projects should focus on developing meaningful use cases for their tokens that align with the project's goals and technology. Utility tokens should serve a purpose within the ecosystem, whether it's enabling access to specific services, participating in governance, or representing ownership in decentralized applications.

Altcoin projects should seek legal counsel from professionals with expertise in cryptocurrency regulations. Legal advisors can help navigate the complex regulatory landscape, provide guidance on compliance obligations, and ensure that the project's operations align with relevant laws.

The altcoin market is dynamic, and regulations can change rapidly. Altcoin projects should remain flexible and adaptable to evolving regulatory developments. Regularly reviewing and updating compliance practices is essential to stay aligned with changing legal requirements.

The future of compliance in the altcoin ecosystem lies in collaboration between industry participants, regulators, and other stakeholders. As the market matures, projects that prioritize compliance, transparency, security, and community engagement are more likely to thrive and contribute positively to the broader cryptocurrency landscape.

Compliance and best practices are foundational pillars for altcoin projects aiming to succeed in the evolving cryptocurrency landscape. By adhering to regulatory requirements, prioritizing transparency, implementing robust security measures, engaging with the community, and aligning with ethical standards, altcoin projects can build trust, attract investment, and drive responsible innovation. In an industry characterized by innovation and rapid change, embracing compliance not only safeguards the project's viability but also contributes to the overall growth and maturation of the altcoin ecosystem.

Potential impacts of regulations on the future of emerging cryptocurrencies

As the landscape of emerging cryptocurrencies evolves, regulatory frameworks have become a central focus for governments, regulatory bodies, and industry stakeholders. The potential impacts of regulations on the future of these innovative digital assets are multifaceted and carry far-reaching implications for market participants, technological development, investor confidence, and the broader financial ecosystem. In this section, we delve into the complex interplay between regulations and emerging cryptocurrencies, exploring the potential effects on innovation, adoption, market dynamics, investor protection, decentralization, and the maturation of the digital finance landscape.

Emerging cryptocurrencies represent a breeding ground for innovation, driving the development of new technologies, use cases, and economic models. Regulatory frameworks have the power to shape the direction of this innovation by providing legal clarity, fostering responsible practices, and mitigating risks. Balancing encouraging innovation and safeguarding against potential abuses is a critical challenge for regulators. Overly stringent regulations could stifle experimentation and technological advancement, while a lack of regulations can expose investors to undue risks. The

lack of regulatory clarity has been a persistent challenge in the cryptocurrency space. Clear and well-defined regulations can provide market participants with a sense of security and predictability, attracting institutional investors and mainstream adoption. Regulatory uncertainty, on the other hand, can deter investment, hinder growth, and contribute to market volatility.

Regulations have the potential to shape the structure of the emerging cryptocurrency market. Regulatory measures such as licensing requirements, AML/KYC regulations, and investor protection mechanisms can enhance market integrity, reduce fraudulent activities, and protect investors from scams. A regulated environment may attract institutional capital while providing retail investors with more confidence to participate.

One of the basic principles of cryptocurrencies is decentralization, allowing for permissionless innovation and financial inclusion. Regulations that impose overly burdensome requirements or restrict access to certain technologies may hinder these principles. Striking a balance between regulation and maintaining the open nature of cryptocurrencies is crucial to preserve the benefits of decentralization.

The decentralized and borderless characteristic of cryptocurrencies presents challenges for global regulatory coordination. However, as governments recognize the international nature of the market, efforts to harmonize regulations across jurisdictions may emerge. International collaboration could establish consistent standards, reduce regulatory arbitrage, and create a more predictable environment for emerging cryptocurrencies to thrive.

Emerging cryptocurrencies span a wide range of use cases beyond traditional finance, including decentralized finance (DeFi), non-fungible tokens (NFTs), and digital identity. Regulations need to be flexible enough to accommodate the diverse functionalities of these assets. Accurate classification of different types of cryptocurrencies based on their utility or security features will play a crucial role in determining their regulatory treatment.

Initial coin offerings (ICOs) and token offerings have been subject to scrutiny due to fraudulent activities and investor losses. Regulatory measures that provide guidelines for conducting transparent and responsible token offerings can enhance investor protection, promote market stability, and encourage legitimate projects to flourish.

The involvement of institutional investors is often seen as a key milestone in the maturation of the cryptocurrency market. Regulatory clarity, custody solutions, and compliance standards are crucial factors in attracting institutional capital. Clear regulations that address concerns such as custody, reporting, and fiduciary responsibilities can open the door to greater institutional participation.
Emerging cryptocurrencies often involve technologies that prioritize privacy, such as zero-knowledge proofs and encryption techniques. Regulations aimed at protecting user data and privacy rights must strike a balance between individual privacy and regulatory oversight, as overly invasive measures could hinder the development of privacy-enhancing technologies.

Regulatory sandboxes, which allow businesses to test innovative solutions under regulatory supervision, have gained traction in various jurisdictions. These sandboxes provide a controlled environment for emerging cryptocurrency projects to develop and iterate on their technologies while ensuring compliance with existing laws.

Decentralized finance (DeFi) platforms have challenged traditional financial intermediaries and regulatory frameworks. As DeFi gains traction, regulators may need to adapt existing regulations to address the unique characteristics of these platforms while preserving their innovative potential.

The potential impacts of regulations on the future of emerging cryptocurrencies are not limited to the short term. Regulatory decisions made today can set the trajectory for the market's growth, development, and integration into the broader financial ecosystem for years to come. The actions taken by regulators and industry stakeholders will shape the narrative of digital finance and its relationship with traditional finance.

The interplay between regulations and emerging cryptocurrencies is a complex and evolving process that will shape the trajectory of the digital finance landscape. The potential impacts of regulations are multidimensional, ranging from fostering innovation, ensuring investor protection, and enhancing market integrity to shaping the role of decentralized technologies, institutional participation, and global standards. Balancing regulation and innovation are paramount to ensure that emerging cryptocurrencies can reach their full potential while contributing positively to the evolution of finance in the digital age.

CHAPTER VI

Navigating the Altcoin Ecosystem

Understanding altcoin exchanges and trading platforms

Altcoin exchanges and trading platforms play a pivotal role in the cryptocurrency ecosystem, serving as the gateway for individuals and institutions to access and trade a diverse array of digital assets beyond Bitcoin. These platforms have evolved significantly since the early days of cryptocurrency, offering various features, trading pairs, and services to provide to the increasing demand for altcoin trading. In this section, we delve into the multifaceted world of altcoin exchanges and trading platforms, exploring their types, functionalities, security measures, liquidity considerations, regulatory challenges, and their role in shaping the future of the altcoin market.

Altcoin exchanges come in various forms, catering to different types of traders and investors. There are centralized exchanges (CEXs) that operate as intermediaries between buyers and sellers, facilitating trades with user-friendly interfaces. On the other hand, decentralized exchanges (DEXs) enable peer-to-peer trading directly from users' wallets, eliminating the need for an intermediary and providing enhanced privacy and security.

Altcoin exchanges offer a wide range of trading pairs that allow users to exchange one cryptocurrency for another.

These pairs can involve popular altcoins, stablecoins, and even Bitcoin as the base currency. Liquidity, or the capacity to purchase or sell an asset quickly without causing significant price fluctuations, is a crucial factor in altcoin trading. Exchanges with higher trading volumes generally have better liquidity, enabling users to execute trades with minimal price slippage.

User experience is a key consideration for altcoin exchanges. Centralized exchanges often provide user-friendly interfaces, making them accessible to both experienced traders and newcomers. Decentralized exchanges, while offering increased privacy and control, may have a sharp learning curve due to their more complex user interfaces.

Security is a paramount concern for altcoin exchanges and trading platforms, as they are often targeted by hackers due to the potential for significant financial gains. Robust security measures, including cold storage for the majority of funds, two-factor authentication (2FA), and encryption, are essential to safeguard user assets. Regular security audits, bug bounty programs, and compliance with industry standards help maintain a secure trading environment.

Altcoin exchanges operate in a regulatory gray area, with the legal status of cryptocurrencies and altcoins varying across jurisdictions. Compliance with anti-money laundering (AML) and know your customer (KYC) regulations is becoming more common in the industry, especially among centralized exchanges. Regulatory uncertainty and evolving requirements pose challenges for exchanges to provide global services while ensuring compliance with regional regulations.

Exchanges play a role in determining which altcoins are listed for trading. Listing decisions involve considerations such as the project's technology, team, use case, community support, and market demand. Some exchanges have introduced evaluation frameworks to assess the potential regulatory implications of listing specific altcoins, contributing to transparency and informed decision-making.

The altcoin market is susceptible to market manipulation due to its relatively low trading volumes and lack of regulations. Exchanges are increasingly investing in market surveillance tools and measures to detect and prevent fraudulent activities, wash trading, and other forms of manipulation that can negatively impact traders and the market's integrity.

In response to market demand, altcoin exchanges have expanded their services beyond spot trading. Margin trading, futures contracts, options trading, and lending platforms have emerged, providing users with a wider range of trading strategies and tools for risk management. These services, while offering opportunities for greater profitability, also come with increased risk due to leverage.

Altcoin exchanges play a critical role in shaping market dynamics by providing a platform for price discovery, liquidity provision, and access to a diverse range of digital assets. They contribute to the overall growth and development of the altcoin market by fostering innovation, enabling trading opportunities, and promoting greater adoption.

Decentralized exchanges (DEXs) align with the core principles of cryptocurrencies by enabling peer-to-peer trading without intermediaries. DEXs provide enhanced privacy and security, but their current limitations in terms of scalability and user experience are challenges that developers are actively addressing to enhance their usability.

The future of altcoin exchanges and trading platforms is likely to be impacted by the advancements in technology, regulatory developments, and market demands. Innovations such as tokenized assets, decentralized liquidity pools, and algorithmic trading mechanisms could reshape the landscape, offering new opportunities for traders and investors.

Altcoin exchanges and trading platforms are the lifelines of the altcoin market, providing traders and investors with the means to access and participate in the dynamic world of cryptocurrencies. From centralized exchanges that offer user-friendly interfaces and higher liquidity to decentralized exchanges that prioritize user control and security, these platforms cater to diverse needs and preferences. As the altcoin market continues to evolve, the role of exchanges in shaping market dynamics, fostering innovation, and adapting to regulatory challenges will remain pivotal in driving the future of the digital finance ecosystem.

Wallet options for storing and securing altcoins

In the world of cryptocurrencies, securing your digital assets is of paramount importance. As the altcoin market expands and diversifies, the need for reliable and secure storage solutions becomes even more critical. Cryptocurrency wallets, which store private keys necessary for accessing and managing digital assets, come in various forms, catering to different levels of security, accessibility, and user preferences. In this section, we explore the diverse landscape of wallet options for storing and securing altcoins, covering categories such as hardware wallets, software wallets, mobile wallets, paper wallets, and the importance of security best practices.

Hardware wallets are commonly considered the gold standard for secure cryptocurrency storage. These physical devices, which resemble USB drives, store private keys offline, minimizing exposure to online threats and hacking attempts. Hardware wallets are immune to malware and phishing attacks that target software wallets. They offer a user-friendly interface for managing and accessing altcoins, with features like multi-currency support and backup options. Popular hardware wallet brands include Ledger and Trezor.

Software wallets encompass a wide range of wallet applications that work on desktop computers or mobile devices. They offer varying levels of security and convenience. Desktop wallets are downloaded on a user's computer, allowing for control over private keys but requiring vigilant security practices to protect against malware and hacking. Mobile wallets, available as apps, provide easy access to altcoins on the go but require careful consideration of device security and backup procedures.

Mobile wallets are designed for smartphones and offer a convenient way to access and manage altcoins. They are particularly suitable for small transactions and daily use. While they offer mobility and ease of use, users must prioritize device security, regularly update the wallet app, and enable necessary security features like PIN codes, biometric authentication, and encryption.

Paper wallets, a type of cold storage solution, involves generating a pair of private and public keys offline and printing them on a physical piece of paper. This approach eliminates the risk of online hacks and malware. However, paper wallets require meticulous precautions to prevent physical loss or damage and should be stored in a secure and protected environment.

Online wallets, often called web wallets, are hosted on the internet by third-party service providers. While they offer convenience and easy accessibility, they also introduce a higher level of risk. Users must trust the security measures of the service provider and be vigilant against potential vulnerabilities. Online wallets are more appropriate for holding small amounts of altcoins for short-term use.

Regardless of the type of wallet chosen, adhering to security best practices is paramount to safeguarding altcoins. These practices include:

Strong Passwords: Use complicated and unique passwords for wallet accounts to minimize the risk of unauthorized access.

Multi-Factor Authentication (MFA): Enable MFA whenever possible to add an further degree of security to your accounts.

Backup and Recovery: Regularly back up your wallet's private keys and recovery phrases in secure offline locations to prevent loss of access due to device failure or theft.

Software Updates: Keep wallet applications and device operating systems updated to protect against security vulnerabilities.

Anti-Malware Software: Use reputable anti-malware software to prevent malware attacks on your devices.

Offline Storage: Store private keys and recovery phrases offline in a secure and encrypted manner.
The diverse range of altcoins presents unique challenges for wallet storage. Not all wallets support every altcoin, and some altcoins have specific wallet requirements. Before choosing a wallet, ensure that it supports the altcoins you intend to store. For altcoins that lack dedicated wallets, consider using hardware wallets that support various cryptocurrencies.

Wallet options also interact with regulatory and privacy considerations. Some wallets that enforce strict know your customer (KYC) procedures can compromise users' privacy. Privacy-focused altcoins might require wallets with enhanced privacy features, such as CoinJoin, to maintain transaction anonymity.
Open source wallets, where the code is publicly available for scrutiny, are generally considered more transparent and secure. Audited wallets, reviewed by security experts, provide an added layer of assurance. Users should prioritize wallets with a strong reputation, active development teams, and a history of prompt security updates.

Educating users about wallet security is a shared responsibility of the cryptocurrency community. Altcoin projects, wallet developers, and exchanges should provide clear guidelines and resources for users to learn about security best practices. Users, in turn, should invest time in understanding the intricacies of wallet security to make informed decisions that protect their digital assets.

Choosing the right wallet for storing and securing altcoins is a crucial step in the journey of cryptocurrency ownership. The diverse range of wallet options available, from hardware wallets that prioritize offline security to mobile wallets that offer convenience, caters to different user preferences and risk tolerances. Regardless of the wallet type chosen, adhering to security best practices, staying informed about potential vulnerabilities, and prioritizing the protection of private keys are vital for keeping the integrity and security of altcoin holdings. As the altcoin market continues to evolve, users' vigilance and responsible wallet management will play a pivotal role in the broader adoption and acceptance of cryptocurrencies in the digital era.

Engaging in token sales and Initial Coin Offerings (ICOs)

Initial Coin Offerings (ICOs) and token sales have revolutionized fundraising in the digital age, offering individuals and investors the opportunity to participate in early-stage projects and gain exposure to innovative blockchain-based ventures. However, the rapid growth of ICOs has also given rise to regulatory challenges, scams, and investor risks. In this section, we explore the concept of ICOs and token sales, covering their benefits, risks, regulatory considerations, due diligence processes, and the evolving landscape of token fundraising.

ICOs and token sales involve the issuance and distribution of digital tokens as a form of fundraising for blockchain-based projects. These tokens often serve a specific utility within the project's ecosystem, such as granting access to services or products. ICOs are typically conducted on blockchain platforms like Ethereum using smart contracts to automate the issuance and distribution of tokens.

ICOs offer several benefits to both project teams and investors. For project teams, ICOs provide a decentralized and efficient means of raising capital without the need for intermediaries. They enable projects to engage a global audience, democratize investment, and gather support from a community of backers who believe in the project's vision. For investors, ICOs offer early access to potentially groundbreaking technologies and the possibility of significant returns on investment if the project succeeds.

ICOs have faced regulatory challenges due to the lack of standardized global regulations and the potential for fraudulent activities. Different jurisdictions classify tokens differently—ranging from securities to utility tokens—and regulations can vary significantly. Regulatory uncertainty can impact project viability, investor confidence, and the overall ICO landscape.

The decentralized nature of ICOs can expose investors to risks, including fraudulent projects, exit scams, and misleading marketing. Scammers have taken advantage of the hype around ICOs to launch fake projects and exploit unsuspecting investors. Conducting thorough due diligence is essential to avoid falling victim to scams. Participating in ICOs requires careful due diligence and research. Investors should assess the project's whitepaper, team credentials, technology, use case, token economics, and community support. Additionally, understanding the project's regulatory compliance efforts, partnerships, and long-term vision is crucial to making informed investment decisions.

The ICO landscape has evolved in response to regulatory concerns. Security Token Offerings (STOs) emerged as a more regulated form of token fundraising, wherein tokens represent ownership in traditional assets like equities or real estate. STOs aim to provide more legal certainty, aligning with existing securities regulations in various jurisdictions.

The concept of tokenomics—the economic model governing the distribution and use of tokens—is central to ICOs. Utility tokens are designed to have intrinsic value within a project's ecosystem, enabling access to goods or services. Tokenomics considerations include token supply, distribution mechanisms, governance features, and potential for token appreciation.

Different token sale models exist to cater to diverse fundraising goals and investor preferences. Crowdsales involve selling tokens to the public, while airdrops distribute tokens to a broader audience for promotional purposes. Private sales, on the other hand, target accredited investors and institutions before the public sale.

Regulatory compliance is vital for the success of ICOs and the protection of investors. Project teams should consider legal opinions, consult experts, and ensure their tokens are properly classified to avoid regulatory pitfalls. Regulatory-compliant projects are more likely to attract institutional investment and long-term community support.

After participating in an ICO, investors must consider the security of their acquired tokens. Storing tokens in secure wallets, following security best practices, and staying informed about potential vulnerabilities are essential steps to prevent loss or theft of tokens.

ICO participants should evaluate a project's long-term vision and commitment to community engagement. Active involvement from the project team, ongoing development, and transparent communication with the community are indicators of a project's dedication to its goals.

Participating in ICOs and token sales offers individuals and investors the opportunity to support cutting-edge projects and gain exposure to the decentralized economy. However, the evolving landscape presents both opportunities and challenges. Navigating the ICO landscape requires a combination of careful due diligence, awareness of regulatory nuances, and adherence to security best practices. By understanding the benefits, risks, and regulatory considerations associated with ICOs, participants can make informed investment decisions that contribute to the growth and innovation of the blockchain ecosystem.

Identifying reputable altcoin projects and avoiding scams

In the dynamic and rapidly evolving world of cryptocurrencies, identifying reputable altcoin projects has become a paramount skill for investors and enthusiasts. The allure of revolutionary technologies, disruptive ideas, and potential financial gains has led to a surge in the number of projects entering the altcoin market. However, this growth has also brought with it a proliferation of scams and fraudulent schemes. In this section, we delve into the art of distinguishing legitimate altcoin projects from scams, exploring strategies for conducting thorough research, recognizing warning signs, assessing project fundamentals, and fostering a culture of responsible investing.

At the core of identifying reputable altcoin projects lies due diligence—an essential process that involves meticulous research and analysis. It begins with understanding the project's whitepaper, a document that outlines its goals, technology, use case, and tokenomics. Reading and comprehending the whitepaper provides valuable insights into the project's objectives and whether it addresses real-world problems.

A reputable altcoin project is often anchored by a skilled and experienced team. Scrutinize the team's profiles, assessing their expertise, professional backgrounds, and accomplishments. Transparent projects provide detailed information about team members, including links to their LinkedIn profiles and contributions to the blockchain community.

A project's utility and real-world applicability are key indicators of its legitimacy. Investigate whether the altcoin addresses a tangible need or offers a novel solution within a specific industry. Projects with clear use cases are more likely to have a long-lasting impact, while those with vague or overly ambitious claims should be approached cautiously.

Reputable altcoin projects maintain transparent and active communication with their communities. Engage with the project's social media channels, online forums, and official communication platforms. Transparent communication demonstrates a commitment to openness, fosters community engagement, and builds investor trust.

The technological foundation of an altcoin project is a vital aspect of its credibility. Assess the project's technology stack, its differentiation from existing solutions, and the feasibility of its implementation. Projects with open-source code, regular updates, and a functional prototype or minimum viable product (MVP) showcase their commitment to technical excellence.

Tokenomics—the economic model governing the distribution and utility of tokens—provides insight into the project's long-term viability. Understand how tokens are used within the project's ecosystem and whether they have genuine utility. A well-balanced tokenomics model discourages speculative behavior and supports the altcoin's sustainable growth.

Legitimate altcoin projects often forge partnerships with established companies, organizations, or industry leaders. These collaborations lend credibility to the project's goals and enhance its chances of success. Investigate the authenticity of partnerships and their potential impact on the project's trajectory.

Navigating the regulatory landscape responsibly is a hallmark of reputable altcoin projects. Projects that seek legal opinions, comply with relevant regulations, and prioritize transparency regarding their regulatory efforts demonstrate a commitment to long-term viability and investor protection.

Recognizing warning signs of scams is crucial for avoiding fraudulent projects. Common red flags include overly aggressive marketing tactics, unrealistic promises of guaranteed returns, a lack of transparency regarding the project's team or technology, and an absence of clear use cases. Be wary of projects that trigger these red flags.

Learning from the mistakes and experiences of others is a valuable strategy for avoiding scams. Research past ICOs that turned out to be fraudulent or failed to deliver on promises. Analyze the factors that led to their downfall and incorporate those lessons into your due diligence process.

The sentiment within the cryptocurrency community can serve as an indicator of a project's reputation. Engage with other investors, participate in discussions, and seek out reviews on reputable platforms. Positive community sentiment often reflects a project's legitimacy and strong community support.

Identifying reputable altcoin projects in a landscape teeming with innovation and potential requires a combination of critical thinking, research, and vigilance. The art of distinguishing between legitimate projects and scams is a skill that empowers investors and supports the health of the altcoin ecosystem. By embracing due diligence, recognizing red flags, and learning from both successes and failures, individuals contribute to a culture of responsible investing that not only safeguards their interests but also fosters the growth of genuinely transformative altcoin projects.

CHAPTER VII

Case Studies and Use Cases

Real-world applications of emerging cryptocurrencies beyond investment

The emergence of cryptocurrencies has ignited a paradigm shift in the technological landscape, extending far beyond their role as speculative assets. While investment remains a prominent aspect of the cryptocurrency ecosystem, the true potential of these digital assets lies in their practical applications across a wide range of industries. In this section, we delve into the multifaceted world of real-world applications for emerging cryptocurrencies, exploring their transformative impact on finance, supply chain management, healthcare, identity verification, voting systems, and more. By understanding how cryptocurrencies and blockchain technology are revolutionizing these sectors, we gain insight into the profound implications these innovations hold for our global society.

The groundbreaking inception of Bitcoin introduced the concept of a decentralized digital currency that works independently of traditional financial intermediaries. Beyond investment, cryptocurrencies are transforming financial systems by enabling secure and swift cross-border transactions at a fraction of the cost incurred by traditional methods. The decentralized nature of blockchain technology underpinning cryptocurrencies ensures transparency, reduces counterparty risk, and provides financial inclusivity to unbanked populations.

In supply chain management, the traceability of goods and products is a longstanding challenge. Cryptocurrencies, coupled with blockchain's transparent and immutable ledger, are revolutionizing supply chain transparency. Businesses can track the journey of products from source to consumer, verifying authenticity, ethical sourcing, and quality along the way. This has profound implications for industries such as fashion, agriculture, and electronics, fostering consumer trust and sustainable practices.

Cryptocurrencies are poised to disrupt the healthcare industry by revolutionizing medical record management. Blockchain technology guarantees the security and integrity of patient data, enabling patients to control access to their medical histories while streamlining information exchange between healthcare providers. This empowers patients to actively manage their healthcare journey and contributes to improved patient outcomes.

Traditional identity verification processes are often cumbersome, time-consuming, and vulnerable to breaches. Cryptocurrencies offer a solution by enabling decentralized identity management. Individuals can control their own identity data, sharing only the necessary information for specific transactions. This has profound implications for border control, financial services, and data privacy, offering individuals greater agency over their personal information.

Election integrity is a cornerstone of democratic societies, yet voter fraud and lack of transparency have persisted as concerns. Emerging cryptocurrencies present a solution through blockchain-based voting systems. These systems provide an immutable record of votes, mitigating the risk of manipulation and enhancing voter participation. By increasing the security and transparency of elections, cryptocurrencies promote the health of democratic institutions.

Intellectual property and copyright issues have plagued content creators for years. Cryptocurrencies offer a novel way to manage ownership and usage rights through blockchain-based digital rights management. Artists, writers, and musicians can ensure fair compensation for their work while preventing unauthorized distribution, effectively reshaping the dynamics of creative industries.

The energy sector is embracing cryptocurrencies to address challenges related to renewable energy adoption and carbon credit verification. Cryptocurrencies facilitate peer-to-peer energy trading, allowing individuals with renewable energy sources to sell excess energy to others in need. Additionally, blockchain ensures the credibility and transparency of carbon credits, encouraging sustainability efforts.

The influence of social media and content platforms in modern society is undeniable. Cryptocurrencies are ushering in a new era of decentralized social media and content platforms. These platforms empower users by granting them ownership of their data, enabling them to earn rewards for engagement, and addressing concerns about content censorship and privacy.

Cross-border remittances have historically been plagued by high fees and slow processing times. Cryptocurrencies offer a transformative solution by enabling near-instant, low-cost, and borderless transactions. Individuals can send funds to family and friends across the globe without the need for intermediaries, thereby enhancing financial accessibility.

Virtual economies within online gaming have evolved into substantial ecosystems with their own currencies and trading dynamics. Cryptocurrencies are amplifying this trend by allowing players to purchase, sell, and trade in-game items using digital tokens. This innovation enhances player engagement and introduces a new dimension of economic interaction within virtual worlds.

While the financial aspect of cryptocurrencies often takes center stage, their practical applications are unlocking a new era of innovation and efficiency across diverse industries. From revolutionizing financial systems and supply chains to transforming healthcare, identity verification, voting, and content creation, cryptocurrencies are proving their value as transformative technologies. As society embraces these innovations, it is imperative to recognize that the impact of emerging cryptocurrencies extends well beyond investment, ushering in a future where transparency, security, and efficiency reshape the foundations of various sectors.

DeFi (Decentralized Finance) and its impact on the altcoin market

The appearance of cryptocurrencies and blockchain technology has sparked a wave of innovation that transcends traditional financial systems. At the forefront of this revolution is Decentralized Finance (DeFi), a movement that seeks to recreate and enhance various financial services using blockchain's inherent decentralization, transparency, and programmability. DeFi has rapidly evolved into a prominent force within the cryptocurrency ecosystem, driving the adoption and proliferation of altcoins—cryptocurrencies other than Bitcoin. In this section, we delve into the concept of DeFi, explore its impact on the altcoin market, and analyze its role in reshaping the financial landscape.

DeFi represents a paradigm shift in the way financial services are accessed, utilized, and interacted with. Traditional finance is characterized by centralized intermediaries, lengthy transaction processes, and restricted access for underserved populations. DeFi leverages blockchain technology to create a decentralized financial ecosystem where users can access services such as lending, borrowing, trading, and yield farming without relying on intermediaries like banks or brokerages. Smart contracts, self-executing code on blockchains, automate and execute financial agreements, ensuring trust and efficiency.

A cornerstone of DeFi is the emergence of platforms built on blockchain networks, most notably Ethereum. These platforms provide various services that mirror traditional financial instruments. For instance, lending protocols like Aave and Compound enable users to lend their assets and earn interest, while decentralized exchanges (DEXs) like Uniswap facilitate peer-to-peer trading without the need for a centralized order book. These platforms, fueled by a diverse array of altcoins, have gained immense popularity due to their accessibility, transparency, and ability to circumvent traditional gatekeepers.

DeFi's rise has significantly impacted the altcoin market by catalyzing innovation and altering market dynamics. Many altcoins have been developed specifically to serve as tokens within the DeFi ecosystem, offering various functionalities and governance rights. These tokens, often referred to as "utility tokens," have utility within specific

DeFi platforms and can be staked, traded, or used to participate in governance decisions. This has created a symbiotic relationship between DeFi and altcoins, where the success of one contributes to the growth of the other.

DeFi's impact on the altcoin market is characterized by the accelerated pace of innovation and experimentation. Altcoin projects now have a platform to showcase their unique use cases and capabilities within the DeFi ecosystem. This has led to the development of altcoins focused on decentralized lending, prediction markets, insurance, stablecoins, and more. The convergence of altcoins and DeFi has fueled creativity, with projects striving to solve existing financial challenges and deliver new opportunities for users.

DeFi has amplified the diversification opportunities for investors within the altcoin market. Traditional cryptocurrencies like Bitcoin and Ethereum once dominated portfolios. However, with the rise of DeFi, a wide array of altcoins has gained prominence, enabling investors to diversify their holdings and participate in innovative projects with potential for high returns. This diversification is not only driven by speculative interest but also by the utility and functionalities that altcoins bring to the DeFi ecosystem.

While DeFi's impact on the altcoin market is undeniably transformative, it also brings forth challenges and risks. The fast-paced nature of DeFi development can result in vulnerabilities and security risks. Smart contract bugs, hacks, and rug pulls—where projects exit with investor funds—are common concerns. Investors and participants must conduct thorough due diligence and understand the risks associated with altcoins and DeFi platforms.

As DeFi blurs the lines between traditional finance and the cryptocurrency space, regulatory challenges emerge. The lack of clear regulatory frameworks poses uncertainties for both altcoins and DeFi platforms. Regulatory actions could impact the adoption and growth of DeFi, influencing the altcoin market dynamics.

The future of the altcoin market within the DeFi landscape lies in integration and collaboration. Altcoin projects that align their offerings with the needs of DeFi platforms are likely to experience increased adoption. Moreover, collaboration between different altcoin projects and DeFi platforms can result in synergistic benefits, offering users a comprehensive suite of financial services.

DeFi's impact on the altcoin market is a testament to the transformative ability of blockchain technology. As DeFi platforms reshape traditional financial services, altcoins are crucial in providing the necessary tools, functionalities, and diversity within this burgeoning ecosystem. DeFi's rise has led to increased adoption and recognition of altcoins, driving innovation, diversification, and investment opportunities. However, participants must remain cautious, conduct thorough research, and navigate the evolving regulatory landscape. As the DeFi-alts nexus continues to evolve, it holds the promise of a more open, efficient, and decentralized financial future.

NFTs (Non-Fungible Tokens) and their role in the emerging cryptocurrency space

In the expansive realm of emerging cryptocurrencies, one innovation has captivated the world's attention: Non-Fungible Tokens (NFTs). These unique digital assets have ushered in a new era of ownership, value, and artistic expression within the digital landscape. NFTs indicate a paradigm shift in how we perceive and interact with digital creations, providing a way to tokenize and authenticate digital items that were previously challenging to monetize. As we delve into the intricacies of NFTs, their impact on the emerging cryptocurrency space becomes increasingly evident, with profound implications for creators, collectors, gamers, and the broader creative economy.

NFTs distinguish themselves from traditional cryptocurrencies like Bitcoin and Ethereum by embodying non-fungibility. While Bitcoin and Ethereum are interchangeable on a one-to-one basis, NFTs are indivisible and unique. This distinctiveness is rooted in blockchain technology, the underlying foundation of NFTs, which ensures the scarcity, provenance, and immutability of each digital asset. This uniqueness has paved the way for a multitude of applications that extend far beyond the realm of investment.

At the heart of NFTs lies a transformative force that has reinvigorated the creative economy. Artists, writers, musicians, as well as creators of all kinds have been empowered to directly monetize their digital works in ways previously unattainable. The traditional struggle of artists to monetize their digital creations due to the ease of copying and sharing has been replaced by a revolutionary concept: proven digital ownership through NFTs. With each NFT serving as a verifiable certificate of authenticity, creators can ensure that their work is unique, rare, and inherently valuable.

NFTs have converged the worlds of art, gaming, and collectibles, forging new dimensions of interaction and engagement. Within the gaming industry, NFTs have elevated the status of in-game assets from disposable items to true digital valuables. Gamers can now own characters, weapons, and land within virtual worlds, transcending the limitations of traditional gaming economies. Meanwhile, NFTs have breathed new life into the concept of collectibles, as virtual trading cards, digital pets, and unique items now hold value beyond the virtual realm.

The rapid ascent of NFTs has not been without challenges. The environmental impact of NFTs, particularly on proof-of-work blockchains like Ethereum, has raised concerns about energy consumption. Additionally, the NFT space has witnessed instances of copyright infringement, unauthorized usage, and unethical behavior. However, these challenges also highlight opportunities for innovation and improvement. Scalability solutions, energy-efficient blockchains, and enhanced copyright protection mechanisms are all under exploration to make NFTs more sustainable and secure.

As NFT technology matures and evolves, it is on the cusp of mainstream adoption. The art world is witnessing a revolution as NFT marketplaces become platforms for both established and emerging artists to showcase their work. Celebrities and musicians are leveraging NFTs to establish deeper connections with their fans, while brands are experimenting with NFTs to enhance customer engagement and loyalty. The inclusivity and global reach of NFTs are democratizing access to creative expression, entertainment, and ownership.

The future trajectory of NFTs is poised for expansion and diversification. The rise of layer-two scaling solutions, which aim to alleviate the energy consumption and scalability issues associated with NFTs, demonstrates the commitment to a sustainable NFT ecosystem. NFTs are set to extend their impact beyond art and gaming, with applications in domains such as real estate, ticketing, virtual reality, and even education. Collaborations between artists, developers, and innovators will continue to shape the NFT landscape, defining the boundaries of what is possible within the digital realm.

NFTs have emerged as a defining innovation in the realm of emerging cryptocurrencies, challenging conventional notions of ownership, value, and creative expression. As NFTs reshape industries, empower artists, and redefine digital ownership, they mark a pivotal moment in the intersection of technology and artistry. NFTs have ignited a global conversation about the meaning of authenticity, rarity, and creativity in the digital age. As we navigate the uncharted horizons of NFTs, one thing is certain: they are here to stay, transforming how we perceive, interact with, and derive value from the digital world.

Adoption challenges and potential solutions

The emerging cryptocurrency space has captured the imagination of individuals, industries, and governments alike, promising a future of decentralized finance, secure transactions, and technological disruption. However, the journey towards widespread adoption of cryptocurrencies and blockchain technology is not without its challenges. From technical complexities to regulatory uncertainties, the path to mainstream acceptance is riddled with hurdles that must be overcome. In this section, we delve into the adoption challenges facing the emerging cryptocurrency space and explore potential solutions that can pave the way for a more inclusive, efficient, and integrated future.

One of the most significant challenges hindering the adoption of cryptocurrencies is the inherent technical complexity. For the average individual, setting up wallets, managing private keys, and understanding blockchain mechanisms can be overwhelming. The user experience of interacting with cryptocurrencies must be simplified and streamlined to match the convenience of traditional financial systems. User-friendly interfaces, intuitive applications, and educational resources are essential to bridge the knowledge gap and make cryptocurrency use accessible to a wider audience.

The inherent volatility of cryptocurrencies presents a formidable barrier to adoption, especially in regions where financial stability is a critical concern. The wild price fluctuations associated with cryptocurrencies can deter individuals and businesses from using them for everyday transactions or long-term investments. Stablecoins, which are pegged to real-world assets like fiat currencies, offer a potential solution by providing a stable medium of exchange within the cryptocurrency ecosystem. By mitigating price volatility, stablecoins can encourage practical usage and broader adoption.

Regulatory uncertainties surrounding cryptocurrencies have created a challenging environment for adoption. Varying regulatory approaches globally have led to confusion among businesses and individuals, inhibiting their willingness to engage with cryptocurrencies. Clear and balanced regulatory frameworks that provide legal clarity, consumer protection, and measures to combat illicit activities are essential to foster trust and encourage adoption. Collaboration between governments, industry stakeholders, and regulatory bodies can lead to comprehensive and balanced regulatory regimes.

The specter of security breaches and cyberattacks looms large over the cryptocurrency space. High-profile hacks of exchanges and wallet providers have eroded trust and deterred potential users. Robust security measures, including advanced encryption, multi-factor authentication, and hardware wallets, are crucial to safeguarding user funds and data. Additionally, education about best practices for secure cryptocurrency management is vital to empower users to protect themselves from potential threats.

The lack of interoperability between different blockchains and cryptocurrency networks hampers the seamless movement of assets and data. Siloed ecosystems limit the potential applications and use cases of cryptocurrencies. Solutions like blockchain interoperability protocols and cross-chain bridges are emerging to facilitate the transfer of assets and data across different blockchains. Interoperability can unlock new opportunities for innovation and collaboration, ultimately driving broader adoption.

For cryptocurrencies to truly gain traction, they need to be accepted as a means of payment by a diverse range of merchants. While progress has been made, merchant acceptance of cryptocurrencies remains limited. The development of easy-to-integrate payment solutions and partnerships between cryptocurrency projects and payment processors can incentivize merchants to embrace cryptocurrencies as a viable payment option, thereby increasing their adoption for everyday transactions.

A lack of education and awareness about cryptocurrencies and their potential benefits is a significant hurdle to adoption. Misinformation, misconceptions, and biases can cloud the public perception of cryptocurrencies. Education initiatives, awareness campaigns, and outreach efforts are essential to demystify cryptocurrencies, explain their advantages, and build a knowledgeable user base that can make informed decisions about their use.

The environmental impact of energy-intensive proof-of-work blockchain networks, such as Bitcoin, has drawn criticism and raised questions about the sustainability of cryptocurrency adoption. Transitioning to energy-efficient consensus mechanisms, like proof-of-stake, and supporting projects focused on sustainability and green energy can address these concerns and align cryptocurrencies with global sustainability goals.

Addressing the adoption challenges in the emerging cryptocurrency space requires collaboration among stakeholders from diverse sectors. Industry players, governments, regulators, technologists, and consumers must work together to develop holistic solutions. Initiatives like sandbox environments for testing innovative blockchain projects, international regulatory collaboration, and educational campaigns can collectively contribute to overcoming adoption barriers.

The journey towards widespread adoption of cryptocurrencies and blockchain technology is fraught with challenges, but the potential rewards are immense. By addressing technical complexities, regulatory uncertainties, security concerns, and other barriers, the cryptocurrency space can transform from a niche innovation to a global force that revolutionizes finance, identity management, supply chains, and more. Through collaborative efforts and innovative solutions, the emerging cryptocurrency space has the opportunity to overcome challenges and pave the way for a future that is decentralized, secure, and inclusive.

CHAPTER VIII

Future Trends and Predictions

Emerging cryptocurrency trends to watch in the coming years

The world of cryptocurrencies is a dynamic and rapidly evolving landscape, marked by innovation, disruption, and transformative potential. A variety of new developments in the years to come have the potential to drastically alter the course of blockchain technology and cryptocurrencies. These developments, which range from the development of decentralized finance (DeFi) to the emergence of central bank digital currencies, or CBDCs, offer an indication of the opportunities and difficulties that lie ahead. In this section, we delve into the key emerging cryptocurrency trends that are set to redefine the industry and influence the global economy.

Decentralized Finance, or DeFi, has emerged as a driving force within the cryptocurrency space, revolutionizing traditional financial services through the ability of blockchain technology. In the coming years, the DeFi ecosystem is expected to mature, bringing increased stability, scalability, and security to its platforms and protocols. As more traditional financial instruments, such as derivatives and lending, find their digital counterparts in DeFi, the sector will likely attract institutional players and broader mainstream adoption. Regulatory clarity and improved user interfaces will play a pivotal role in enabling DeFi to achieve its full potential.

Central banks around the world are exploring the introduction of Central Bank Digital Currencies (or CBDCs) as a means to modernize payment systems, enhance financial inclusion, and maintain monetary sovereignty. The coming years are likely to witness the development and implementation of CBDCs, with varying degrees of technological innovation and underlying frameworks. While CBDCs offer advantages in terms of efficiency and traceability, concerns about privacy, data security, and the potential influence on the traditional banking system will need to be addressed.

As the blockchain ecosystem diversifies, interoperability between different blockchain networks becomes increasingly important. Cross-chain solutions, such as interoperability protocols and bridges, are emerging to enable the seamless transfer of assets and data across disparate blockchains. This trend will foster collaboration, innovation, and the creation of interconnected blockchain ecosystems that transcend the limitations of individual networks. Interoperability will unlock new use cases and provide users with greater flexibility in controlling their assets.

The environmental impact of energy-intensive proof-of-work blockchains has drawn attention to the need for sustainability and energy efficiency within the cryptocurrency industry. In response, many projects are transitioning to energy-efficient consensus mechanisms like proof-of-stake. Additionally, the exploration of renewable energy sources for mining operations and the rise of green cryptocurrencies highlight the growing emphasis on environmental responsibility. The convergence of sustainability and blockchain technology will shape the industry's trajectory in the years to come.

Privacy and security remain paramount concerns within the cryptocurrency space. Emerging trends in privacy-focused technologies, such as zero-knowledge proofs and secure multi-party computation, aim to enhance transaction privacy without jeopardizing the integrity of the blockchain. Moreover, advancements in hardware wallets, biometric authentication, and decentralized identity solutions will bolster the security of cryptocurrency holdings and transactions, fostering trust and wider adoption.

The Artificial Intelligence (AI) and blockchain technology integration holds significant potential for creating new synergies and use cases. AI can enhance the efficiency of consensus mechanisms, automate smart contract execution, and optimize blockchain networks. Moreover, the combination of AI and blockchain can facilitate data sharing, provenance verification, and secure digital identity management. Collaborations between these two transformative technologies are likely to yield innovative solutions across industries.

Non-Fungible Tokens (NFTs) have acquired prominence in the realm of digital art and collectibles. However, the trend of NFTs is expected to expand beyond the realm of creativity. NFTs will likely find applications in areas such as real estate, supply chain management, and tokenized ownership of physical assets. This evolution will redefine the concept of ownership and unlock novel opportunities for fractional ownership and liquidity.

Cryptocurrencies have the potential to revolutionize cross-border remittances, enabling faster, cheaper, and more inclusive transactions. In regions with insuffiecient access to traditional financial services, cryptocurrencies can provide avenues for financial inclusion and economic empowerment. As blockchain infrastructure improves and regulatory frameworks become clearer, cross-border remittances using cryptocurrencies will gain traction, benefiting individuals and economies alike.

The trend of tokenization, which involves representing real-world assets as digital tokens on blockchains, is poised to gain momentum. Assets like real estate, stocks, commodities, and intellectual property can be tokenized, enabling fractional ownership and enhancing liquidity. This trend will democratize access to investment opportunities and enable individuals to diversify their portfolios beyond traditional assets.

Regulatory frameworks for cryptocurrencies and blockchain technology are evolving, as governments grapple with the challenges and opportunities presented by these innovations. The coming years are likely to witness increased regulatory clarity and recognition of cryptocurrencies as legitimate financial instruments. Collaborative efforts between industry stakeholders and regulators will contribute to fostering a balanced regulatory environment that promotes innovation while safeguarding consumer interests.

The emerging cryptocurrency trends outlined in this essay offer a glimpse into a dynamic and transformative future. From the maturation of DeFi to the evolution of CBDCs, the integration of AI and blockchain, and the continued rise of tokenization, the cryptocurrency landscape is poised for further disruption and innovation. While challenges such as regulatory uncertainties and security concerns persist, the potential benefits in terms of financial inclusion, efficiency, and empowerment are undeniable. As the years unfold, the interplay of these trends will shape the trajectory of cryptocurrencies and blockchain technology, impacting industries, economies, and societies on a global scale.

The role of altcoins in the evolving financial ecosystem

The emergence of cryptocurrencies has sparked a paradigm shift in the financial landscape, challenging traditional models of currency, payment systems, and value exchange. While Bitcoin, as the pioneering cryptocurrency, laid the foundation for this revolution, it paved the way for the rise of a multitude of alternative cryptocurrencies, commonly known as altcoins. These altcoins, each with its unique features, use cases, and underlying technologies, have catalyzed the transformation of the financial ecosystem into a dynamic and diverse landscape. In this section, we delve into the role of altcoins in the evolving financial ecosystem, exploring their contributions, challenges, and the broader implications they hold for the future of finance.

Altcoins play a crucial role in diversifying the cryptocurrency ecosystem beyond the dominance of Bitcoin. While Bitcoin serves as the flagship cryptocurrency and digital gold, altcoins offer specialized functionalities and use cases that address specific needs and challenges. Ethereum, for instance, introduced the concept of smart contracts, allowing the creation of decentralized applications and programmable assets. Other altcoins, such as Ripple (XRP) and Litecoin (LTC), focus on facilitating faster cross-border transactions and enhancing scalability, respectively. This diversification provides users with a range of options tailored to their preferences, driving innovation and expanding the scope of cryptocurrency applications.

Altcoins are at the forefront of technological innovation within the cryptocurrency space. While Bitcoin introduced the concept of blockchain and proof-of-work consensus mechanisms, altcoins have experimented with various consensus mechanisms, such as proof-of-stake, delegated proof-of-stake, and practical Byzantine fault tolerance. These innovations aim to address scalability, energy efficiency, and security concerns associated with the original blockchain design. Altcoins also drive the exploration of privacy-focused features, interoperability solutions, and enhanced smart contract capabilities. Their experimentation contributes to a collective technological evolution that benefits the entire cryptocurrency ecosystem.

Altcoins are instrumental in exploring niche use cases and real-world applications of blockchain technology. Cryptocurrencies like Monero (XMR) prioritize privacy and anonymity, making them suitable for transactions that require confidentiality. Chainlink (LINK) focuses on decentralized oracle networks, enabling the integration of real-world data into smart contracts. These use cases extend beyond the realm of finance, impacting domains such as supply chain management, healthcare, identity verification, and more. Altcoins thus drive the exploration of blockchain's potential to disrupt and improve various industries.

Altcoins contribute to the broader mission of financial inclusion by giving underserved and unbanked populations an access to financial services. Traditional financial systems often exclude individuals who lack access to banking infrastructure. Altcoins can be accessed and utilized by anyone with an internet connection, enabling individuals in remote or marginalized areas to participate in the global economy. Projects like Stellar (XLM) and Ripple (XRP) aim to facilitate cross-border payments and remittances, offering a more cost-effective and efficient substitute to traditional remittance channels.

Altcoins embody a culture of experimentation and risk-taking within the cryptocurrency community. While not all altcoin projects succeed, the process of innovation and competition drives the industry forward. New ideas, technologies, and approaches are tested through altcoin projects, pushing the boundaries of what is possible within the cryptocurrency ecosystem. This culture of experimentation fosters an environment where lessons learned from successes and failures contribute to the collective knowledge base, ultimately benefitting the industry as a whole.

While altcoins offer numerous benefits, they also pose challenges that must be acknowledged. The altcoin market is rife with scams, pump-and-dump schemes, and projects with little to no utility. The lack of regulatory oversight in some cases can lead to fraudulent activities that harm unsuspecting investors. Additionally, the rapid proliferation of altcoins can make it challenging for investors to distinguish between legitimate projects and those with dubious intentions. Thus, investors must exercise caution and conduct thorough research before engaging with any altcoin project.

Altcoins are gradually gaining recognition and integration within traditional financial systems. Institutional interest in cryptocurrencies has led to the inclusion of select altcoins in investment portfolios and funds. Moreover, the development of financial products like cryptocurrency derivatives and futures contracts demonstrates the evolving interaction between traditional finance and the cryptocurrency market. As altcoins mature and gain acceptance, their integration into mainstream financial services and products is likely to increase.

Altcoins are not merely isolated entities; they are integral to the broader transformation of the global financial landscape. Their innovation, experimentation, and disruption challenge conventional financial norms and systems. As altcoins evolve and prove their value, they contribute to shaping a future where financial transactions, assets, and value exchange are decentralized, efficient, and accessible on a global scale.

The role of altcoins in the evolving financial ecosystem is multifaceted and dynamic. From diversification and innovation to niche use cases and financial inclusion, altcoins are driving the cryptocurrency industry forward. However, with these opportunities come challenges, such as the need for regulatory clarity and discernment among investors. As altcoins continue to evolve, they contribute to a financial landscape that is more diverse, technologically advanced, and inclusive. Ultimately, the contributions of altcoins are pivotal in reshaping the way we conceive of, interact with, and participate in the global economy.

Potential disruptions caused by emerging cryptocurrencies

The emergence of cryptocurrencies has ignited a technological revolution with the power to reshape industries, economies, and societies. While Bitcoin laid the foundation for this transformative journey, it is the influx of emerging cryptocurrencies—each with its unique attributes and capabilities—that holds the potential to disrupt established norms and systems. From finance and supply chains to governance and identity management, the impact of emerging cryptocurrencies reaches far and wide. In this section, we explore the potential disruptions caused by emerging cryptocurrencies and examine their implications for the future.

One of the most notable disruptions driven by emerging cryptocurrencies is the rise of decentralized finance (DeFi). DeFi leverages blockchain technology to recreate traditional financial services, such as lending, borrowing, and trading, in a decentralized and permissionless manner. The ability to participate in financial activities without intermediaries has the potential to democratize access to financial services, particularly in regions with limited banking infrastructure. However, this disruption raises questions about consumer protection, regulatory oversight, and the potential for systemic risks if not properly managed.

Emerging cryptocurrencies have the potential to revolutionize cross-border payments and remittances, addressing longstanding challenges in speed, cost, and accessibility. Cryptocurrencies like Ripple (XRP) and Stellar (XLM) enable near-instant cross-border transactions, bypassing traditional correspondent banking networks. This disruption has the potential to empower individuals and businesses by reducing fees and settlement times. Nevertheless, regulatory concerns, volatility, and the need for seamless integration with existing financial systems remain obstacles to realizing the full potential of cryptocurrency-powered remittances. Blockchain-based emerging cryptocurrencies are driving disruptions in supply chain management by enhancing transparency, traceability, and efficiency. Cryptocurrencies like VeChain (VET) enable the tracking of goods from source to destination, reducing counterfeiting, fraud, and supply chain inefficiencies. This innovation ensures greater consumer confidence and accountability across industries, yet the implementation of such disruptions requires collaboration among stakeholders, standardization of protocols, and overcoming technical challenges.

The decentralization offered by emerging cryptocurrencies is challenging conventional identity management systems. Self-sovereign identity solutions, powered by blockchain technology, enable individuals to control their personal information securely and selectively share it when needed. This disruption holds the potential to combat identity theft, enhance privacy, and streamline user verification processes. However, regulatory frameworks, interoperability issues, and public adoption are essential factors that must be addressed for the successful integration of decentralized identity solutions.

Emerging cryptocurrencies, in conjunction with Non-Fungible Tokens (NFTs), are reshaping how content creators, artists, and intellectual property owners monetize their creations. NFTs represent unique digital assets, allowing creators to assert ownership and authenticity over digital art, collectibles, and virtual real estate. This disruption empowers creators to directly monetize their work and engage with audiences, bypassing traditional intermediaries. Nevertheless, concerns about copyright infringement, the environmental impact of energy-intensive networks, and the speculative nature of NFT markets persist. Blockchain-enabled cryptocurrencies are introducing novel solutions for secure and transparent voting systems, transforming governance structures at various levels. Decentralized platforms allow users to participate in decision-making processes, transcending geographical boundaries. This disruption has the potential to enhance inclusivity, reduce voter fraud, and increase civic engagement. However, implementing secure and scalable decentralized voting systems requires addressing challenges related to identity verification, accessibility, and ensuring the integrity of the voting process.

The disruption caused by emerging cryptocurrencies extends to the energy sector. Cryptocurrencies like Bitcoin have been criticized for their energy-intensive proof-of-work consensus mechanisms. Emerging alternatives, such as proof-of-stake and delegated proof-of-stake, offer more energy-efficient alternatives that align with sustainability goals. By incentivizing miners or validators with cryptocurrency stakes rather than computational power, these consensus mechanisms address environmental concerns while enabling blockchain networks to function securely.

The rise of microtransactions facilitated by cryptocurrencies has the potential to reshape the way digital content is monetized. Content creators, journalists, and online platforms can leverage cryptocurrencies to receive micropayments directly from consumers for access to articles, videos, music, and other digital content. This disruption challenges traditional paywall models and advertising-based revenue streams. However, the scalability of blockchain networks and the adoption of micropayment solutions by mainstream audiences are crucial factors that will influence the success of this disruption.

Emerging cryptocurrencies hold promise in addressing financial inclusion by providing unbanked and underbanked populations access to financial services. Cryptocurrencies enable individuals to access savings, credit, and investment opportunities through mobile devices. This disruption has the potential to empower individuals in regions with limited banking infrastructure, fostering economic growth and reducing inequality. Yet, challenges such as regulatory uncertainty, technological literacy, and security concerns must be navigated to ensure that this disruption benefits the most vulnerable populations.

While the disruptions caused by emerging cryptocurrencies offer promising solutions to various challenges, they are not without their share of obstacles. Regulatory frameworks, technological scalability, interoperability, and cybersecurity remain critical considerations for the successful implementation of these disruptions. Additionally, striking a balance between innovation and safeguarding consumer interests is essential to harnessing the transformative power of emerging cryptocurrencies responsibly.

Emerging cryptocurrencies are pioneers of a new era, challenging the status quo and introducing innovative solutions to age-old problems. From transforming financial services to revolutionizing supply chains and governance structures, these disruptions are redefining how we interact, transact, and collaborate. While the journey is accompanied by challenges and uncertainties, the potential for positive change is undeniable. As emerging cryptocurrencies continue to evolve, their impact on industries, economies, and societies will shape the contours of a more decentralized, inclusive, and technologically advanced future.

Speculation on the future landscape of digital assets

The realm of digital assets has rapidly evolved since the inception of Bitcoin, reshaping the way we conceive of value, ownership, and financial systems. As blockchain technology and cryptocurrencies gain broader acceptance, the landscape of digital assets continues to expand, presenting a tantalizing view of what the future might hold. In this section, we embark on a speculative journey to envision the potential landscape of digital assets, exploring the convergence of technology, finance, and society that is likely to shape the trajectory of this transformative domain.

One of the most compelling visions for the future of digital assets is the tokenization of real-world assets. Traditional assets such as real estate, art, commodities, and even intellectual property could be represented by digital tokens on blockchain networks. This would enable fractional ownership, enhance liquidity, and democratize access to assets that were previously illiquid and exclusive. Tokenization has the potential to reshape industries, unlocking new investment opportunities for an extensive array of individuals and facilitating efficient peer-to-peer transactions with reduced intermediaries.

The future landscape of digital assets may see the smooth convergence of the digital and physical worlds. Augmented reality (or AR) and virtual reality (or VR) technologies could enable immersive experiences where digital assets are intertwined with physical environments. Imagine a scenario where owning a digital collectible grants you access to virtual exhibitions or interactive experiences related to the artwork. Such convergence could blur the lines between the tangible and the digital, ushering in novel forms of ownership and interaction.
As blockchain technology advances, digital assets could become programmable money, capable of executing complex financial agreements autonomously through smart contracts. Imagine a mortgage contract that automatically adjusts interest rates based on predefined market conditions or insurance policies that trigger payouts when specific criteria are met. This level of automation could streamline processes, reduce friction,

and enhance transparency in financial transactions. However, this evolution would also require robust security measures and comprehensive legal frameworks to address potential risks and challenges.

The future landscape of digital assets may witness the proliferation of decentralized autonomous organizations (DAOs), where decision-making and governance are driven by token holders. DAOs could reshape corporate structures, enabling more direct participation from stakeholders and aligning incentives with long-term goals. Tokens representing voting rights and ownership within DAOs could redefine notions of corporate governance, fostering greater transparency, accountability, and community involvement in the management of organizations.

Interoperability among different blockchain networks could lead to a future where digital assets can seamlessly move between various ecosystems. This could facilitate the creation of cross-chain assets, allowing users to interact with multiple blockchain platforms while maintaining ownership of their assets. Interoperability would also enable the integration of various functionalities and features, paving the way for more comprehensive and versatile digital asset ecosystems.

The rise of digital assets may see the introduction of central bank digital currencies (CBDCs), issued and regulated by national monetary authorities. CBDCs could coexist with cryptocurrencies and stablecoins, offering governments greater control over monetary policy and enhancing the efficiency of payment systems. However, the integration of CBDCs into existing financial infrastructures poses technical, regulatory, and privacy challenges that must be carefully navigated.

The future landscape of digital assets may place heightened emphasis on security and custodianship solutions. As the value and variety of digital assets grow, innovative approaches to securing private keys, mitigating risks, and providing insurance coverage could become essential components of the ecosystem. Additionally, advancements in encryption and multi-factor authentication could enhance the security of digital assets, fostering greater confidence among investors and users.

The sustainability of digital assets could be a significant consideration in the future landscape. The growing awareness of environmental concerns related to energy-intensive proof-of-work consensus mechanisms could drive the adoption of more energy-efficient alternatives, such as proof-of-stake and proof-of-authority. Furthermore, projects focused on carbon-neutral or carbon-negative blockchain solutions could align digital asset technology with broader sustainability goals.

The future of digital assets will likely be shaped by the development of regulatory frameworks that balance innovation along with consumer protection and financial stability. International collaboration will be crucial to harmonize regulations across borders, facilitating the responsible growth of the digital asset ecosystem. Clear regulatory guidelines could attract institutional investors, stimulate innovation, and promote healthy competition in the global digital asset market.

The overarching theme in the future landscape of digital assets could be the democratization of finance and inclusion. As digital assets enable broader access to financial services, ownership, and investment opportunities, individuals from diverse backgrounds could participate in the global economy on more equitable terms. This democratization has the potential to reshape traditional power dynamics, reduce financial inequalities, and unlock untapped economic potential.

The speculative landscape of digital assets presents a vision that extends beyond the horizon, driven by technological advancement, societal needs, and human creativity. While the future is uncertain, the potential disruptions brought about by digital assets are profound. From reimagining ownership to enhancing financial inclusivity, the convergence of technology and finance is paving the way for a future where digital assets play an integral role in shaping economies and societies worldwide. As we navigate this uncharted territory, responsible innovation, collaboration, and a commitment to equitable access will be vital to realize the transformative potential of digital assets in a rapidly evolving world.

CONCLUSION

Recap of key points discussed in the e-book

Throughout this comprehensive e-book, we've embarked on a journey through the intricate and dynamic world of cryptocurrencies and emerging digital assets. Our exploration has covered a wide range of topics, from the foundational concepts of altcoins to the potential disruptions they bring to the financial ecosystem. As we conclude this e-book, let's recap the key points we've discussed, providing a holistic overview of the insights gained.

In the introduction, we delved into the significance of altcoins in the evolving landscape of digital assets. We defined altcoins as cryptocurrencies other than Bitcoin and highlighted their diverse applications and potential for reshaping traditional financial systems. The introduction set the stage for our deep dive into the multifaceted aspects of altcoins.

Definition of Altcoins and Their Role in the Crypto Landscape
In our exploration of altcoins, we defined them as cryptocurrencies that are developed as alternatives to Bitcoin, each with distinct features and use cases. We discussed the importance of altcoins in diversifying the cryptocurrency ecosystem, fostering innovation, and addressing limitations present in Bitcoin. The discussion also emphasized the categorization of altcoins into forks, tokens, stablecoins, privacy coins, and more.

Historical Context: The Rise of Bitcoin and the Need for Alternative Cryptocurrencies

The historical context provided insight into the rise of Bitcoin as the pioneering cryptocurrency. We examined the motivations for creating alternative cryptocurrencies and how they aimed to overcome the limitations of Bitcoin, such as scalability and privacy concerns. This historical perspective highlighted the iterative nature of cryptocurrency development and the ongoing pursuit of innovation.

Categories of Altcoins: Forks, Tokens, Stablecoins, Privacy Coins, etc.
Our exploration into the categories of altcoins deepened our understanding of the diverse range of cryptocurrencies. We discussed forks, which are created through modifications to existing blockchain protocols, and tokens, which are built on established blockchain platforms. We explored stablecoins designed to mitigate price volatility and privacy coins focused on enhancing transaction anonymity. This comprehensive overview underscored the innovation and versatility within the altcoin space.

Pros and Cons of Investing in Altcoins

Investment considerations took center stage as we explored the benefits and drawbacks of investing in altcoins. We discussed the potential for higher returns due to the volatility of altcoin markets and the opportunity for diversification. However, we also emphasized the associated risks, such as market volatility, regulatory uncertainty, and the presence of fraudulent projects. A balanced perspective on investment strategies and risk management was highlighted.

What Constitutes an Emerging Cryptocurrency?

Our examination of emerging cryptocurrencies led us to define them as new digital assets with innovative features, use cases, and technologies. We explored how these emerging projects seek to address real-world difficulties and push the boundaries of blockchain technology. The discussion illuminated the dynamic nature of the cryptocurrency landscape, where constant innovation paves the way for new opportunities.

Factors Driving the Emergence of New Cryptocurrencies

The emergence of new cryptocurrencies is fueled by a multitude of factors that we meticulously examined. Technological advancements, the pursuit of scalability, and the desire for enhanced privacy were among the driving forces. We discussed how global economic trends, regulatory developments, and shifts in investor sentiment contribute to the rise of emerging cryptocurrencies. These factors collectively shape the trajectory of the digital asset ecosystem.

Case Studies of Successful Emerging Cryptocurrencies (e.g., Ethereum, Cardano, Solana)
Our exploration of case studies provided insights into the success stories of notable emerging cryptocurrencies. Ethereum's groundbreaking smart contract capabilities, Cardano's focus on research-driven development, and Solana's high-performance blockchain were analyzed in detail. These case studies exemplified the potential of

emerging cryptocurrencies to disrupt industries and drive innovation.

Challenges Faced by Emerging Cryptocurrencies

We delved into the challenges faced by emerging cryptocurrencies, including technological hurdles, regulatory uncertainties, and competition within the crowded market. Scalability issues, network security concerns, and the need for user-friendly interfaces were explored. Additionally, regulatory compliance, public adoption, and maintaining decentralized principles were identified as ongoing challenges that projects must navigate.

Smart Contracts and Their Significance in the Technology Behind Emerging Cryptocurrencies
Our exploration of technology behind emerging cryptocurrencies led us to examine the significance of smart contracts. We discussed how smart contracts are self-executing agreements that automate processes and transactions on blockchain platforms. Ethereum's role in popularizing smart contracts was emphasized, along with its potential to revolutionize industries beyond finance, like supply chain management and digital identity verification.

Consensus Mechanisms: PoW vs. PoS vs. Others

The exploration of consensus mechanisms provided an in-depth comparison of proof of work (PoW) and proof of stake (PoS) protocols. We discussed how PoW, employed by Bitcoin, relies on computational power, while PoS, adopted by emerging projects like Ethereum 2.0 and Cardano, utilizes token ownership for network validation.

We also touched on other consensus mechanisms, highlighting their impact on security, energy efficiency, and decentralization.

Interoperability and Scalability Solutions in Emerging Cryptocurrencies

The significance of interoperability and scalability solutions was explored, addressing the challenges of blockchain networks' limited transaction throughput and the need for seamless communication between different platforms. We discussed projects like Polkadot and Cosmos that aim to bridge blockchains and enable data and asset transfers across ecosystems. Scalability solutions, such as layer-2 protocols and sharding, were also examined for their potential to enhance network performance.

Innovation in Blockchain Technology within the Emerging Cryptocurrency Space

Our exploration into innovation within the emerging cryptocurrency space highlighted the continuous development of novel technologies. We discussed projects working on enhancing privacy, introducing new consensus mechanisms, and experimenting with novel governance models. The discussion emphasized the iterative nature of blockchain development, with emerging projects pushing boundaries and introducing features that can redefine industries.

Risk Assessment and Risk Management in Altcoin Investments

The significance of risk assessment and management in altcoin investments was underscored. We examined methods for evaluating project fundamentals, team credibility, technological viability, and market trends. We emphasized the need for due diligence and diversification to mitigate risks associated with volatile markets and regulatory uncertainties. The role of risk management strategies and long-term perspectives in navigating the altcoin investment landscape was highlighted.

Fundamental Analysis of Emerging Cryptocurrencies

Our exploration of fundamental analysis underscored its significance in evaluating the potential of emerging cryptocurrencies. We discussed factors such as the project's technology, use case, market demand, team expertise, and competitive landscape. Fundamental analysis provides a holistic perspective that helps investors make informed decisions and identify projects with the potential for sustainable growth.

Technical Analysis and Chart Patterns for Altcoin Trading

Technical analysis emerged as a vital tool for altcoin trading, focusing on historical price data, chart patterns, and market trends. We explored concepts such as support and resistance levels, moving averages, and indicators like the Relative Strength Index (RSI). The discussion emphasized the complementary nature of technical analysis and fundamental analysis, aiding traders in making well-rounded decisions.

Diversification and Portfolio Management for Altcoin Trading

Diversification and portfolio management strategies were discussed as essential approaches to mitigating risk in altcoin trading. We explored concepts like asset allocation, risk tolerance assessment, and the role of long-term investment principles. The discussion highlighted the importance of a balanced portfolio that accounts for different risk profiles and potential rewards, aligning with an individual's investment goals.

Global Regulatory Trends for Cryptocurrencies and Altcoins

The complex landscape of global regulatory trends was explored, highlighting the diverse approaches countries have taken toward cryptocurrencies and altcoins. We discussed the challenges of achieving regulatory clarity, investor protection, and fostering innovation while preventing illicit activities. The discussion emphasized the need for collaboration between industry stakeholders and regulatory bodies to strike a balance that promotes responsible growth.

Legal Challenges and Uncertainties in the Altcoin Market

We delved into the legal challenges and uncertainties facing the altcoin market, such as the classification of tokens, securities regulations, and the application of existing financial laws to digital assets. The discussion highlighted the evolving nature of legal frameworks, the importance of compliance, and the role of regulatory sandboxes in fostering innovation while ensuring consumer protection.

Compliance and Best Practices for Altcoin Projects

The significance of compliance and best practices in altcoin projects was examined, focusing on transparency, regulatory adherence, and ethical conduct. We discussed how projects can adopt industry standards, implement

Know Your Customer (KYC) and Anti-Money Laundering (AML) procedures, and prioritize security measures. By following these practices, projects can build trust, attract investors, and contribute to the legitimacy of the digital asset ecosystem.

Potential Impacts of Regulations on the Future of Emerging Cryptocurrencies
The potential impacts of regulations on the future of emerging cryptocurrencies were explored in-depth. We discussed scenarios where favorable regulations could stimulate innovation, attract institutional investment, and foster mainstream adoption. Conversely, excessive regulations or a lack of regulatory clarity could stifle growth and innovation. The discussion underscored the importance of regulatory environments that balance innovation and consumer protection.

Understanding Altcoin Exchanges and Trading Platforms

We explored the world of altcoin exchanges and trading platforms, discussing how they facilitate the buying, selling, and trading of digital assets. We emphasized the importance of security, user experience, liquidity, and regulatory compliance when choosing an exchange. The discussion highlighted the role of centralized and decentralized exchanges in providing access to a variety of altcoins.

Wallet Options for Storing and Securing Altcoins

The significance of wallet options for storing and securing altcoins was examined, emphasizing the differences between hot wallets (online) and cold wallets (offline). We explored hardware wallets, software wallets, and paper wallets, discussing the importance of private key management and best practices for safeguarding digital assets. The discussion underscored the critical role of security in protecting assets from cyber threats.

Engaging in Initial Coin Offerings (ICOs) and Token Sales

We examined the process of participating in Initial Coin Offerings (ICOs) and token sales, emphasizing the importance of due diligence and cautious investment practices. We discussed how ICOs provide funding for projects in exchange for tokens, while Security Token Offerings (STOs) comply with regulatory requirements. The discussion highlighted the risks associated with token sales and the need for proper research before investing.

Identifying Reputable Altcoin Projects and Avoiding Scams

Our exploration into identifying reputable altcoin projects and avoiding scams emphasized the importance of research, critical thinking, and skepticism. We discussed red flags, such as promises of unrealistic returns, lack of transparency, and absence of a credible team. The discussion underscored the significance of community engagement, verified information, and expert analysis in making informed decisions.

Real-World Applications of Emerging Cryptocurrencies Beyond Investment

We explored the real-world applications of emerging cryptocurrencies beyond investment, focusing on areas such as supply chain management, identity verification, content ownership, and voting systems. We discussed how blockchain technology enhances transparency, traceability, and efficiency in these domains, disrupting traditional practices and fostering innovation.

DeFi (Decentralized Finance) and Its Impact on the Altcoin Market
Decentralized Finance (DeFi) emerged as a transformative force, reshaping the altcoin market. We explored how DeFi projects enable peer-to-peer lending, borrowing, trading, and yield farming through smart contracts. The discussion highlighted the potential of DeFi to democratize financial services, enhance liquidity, and introduce new investment opportunities.

NFTs (Non-Fungible Tokens) and Their Role in the Emerging Cryptocurrency Space
Non-Fungible Tokens (NFTs) took center stage as we explored their role in the emerging cryptocurrency space. We discussed how NFTs represent unique digital assets, enabling ownership of digital art, collectibles, and virtual real estate. The discussion emphasized the intersection of NFTs with art, entertainment, gaming, and more, while also examining concerns about copyright and environmental impact.

Adoption Challenges and Potential Solutions in the Emerging Cryptocurrency Space
Adoption challenges and potential solutions were examined, focusing on factors such as user experience, technological literacy, and regulatory clarity. We discussed the need for user-friendly interfaces, scalable solutions, and education initiatives to bridge the gap between the general public and emerging cryptocurrencies. The discussion underscored the

importance of collaboration among industry stakeholders to drive widespread adoption.

Emerging Cryptocurrency Trends to Watch in the Coming Years

Our exploration of emerging cryptocurrency trends highlighted the potential disruptions and advancements to anticipate in the near future. We discussed tokenization of assets, the role of decentralized finance, the evolution of central bank digital currencies (CBDCs), and the ongoing impact of regulatory developments. The discussion illuminated the transformative potential of digital assets across various sectors.

The Role of Altcoins in the Evolving Financial Ecosystem

We explored the crucial role of altcoins in the evolving financial ecosystem, emphasizing their potential to democratize access to financial services, challenge traditional institutions, and enable innovative use cases. We discussed how altcoins contribute to financial inclusivity, cross-border transactions, and the reimagining of ownership paradigms. The discussion underscored the diversified future of finance driven by altcoins.

Potential Disruptions Caused by Emerging Cryptocurrencies

Potential disruptions caused by emerging cryptocurrencies were analyzed, spanning financial systems, supply chains, healthcare, governance, and more. We discussed how blockchain technology and altcoins are reshaping established paradigms, enabling new business models, and fostering greater transparency.

The discussion emphasized the transformative impact on various sectors and the need for adaptability.

Speculation on the Future Landscape of Digital Assets

In the speculative exploration of the future landscape of digital assets, we envisioned tokenization of real-world assets, the convergence of digital and physical realms, and the impact of programmable money through smart contracts. We discussed the rise of decentralized autonomous organizations (DAOs), interoperability solutions, and potential advancements in sustainability and security. The discussion highlighted the transformative potential of these trends.

As we conclude this e-book, we have traversed a rich and dynamic landscape, from the foundational concepts to the speculative horizons of the digital asset ecosystem. The convergence of technology, finance, and society continues to drive the evolution of altcoins and emerging cryptocurrencies, fostering innovation, challenging traditional norms, and redefining how we perceive value, ownership, and financial systems. As the journey into this transformative space continues, it is imperative to remain vigilant, open to change, and committed to responsible innovation that aligns with the broader goals of a connected and inclusive global economy.

Encouragement for readers to continue learning and staying updated

As we conclude this comprehensive exploration of altcoins and emerging cryptocurrencies, we invite you, the readers, to embark on an onging journey of learning and staying updated in this rapidly evolving domain. The world of digital assets is dynamic, transformative, and filled with opportunities that can reshape industries, economies, and even the way we interact with technology. In this section, we offer encouragement and guidance to inspire you to dive deeper, embrace innovation, and remain engaged in the ongoing evolution of the cryptocurrency landscape.

The journey into the world of altcoins and emerging cryptocurrencies is a never-ending quest for knowledge. Embrace the spirit of lifelong learning, recognizing that the digital asset ecosystem is characterized by rapid advancements, paradigm shifts, and constant innovation. Stay curious, seek out reputable sources of information, and cultivate a mindset of continuous growth. Whether you're an investor, a technologist, or simply an enthusiast, staying informed will empower you to make knowledgeable decisions and actively contribute to the transformation unfolding around us.

In a space as dynamic and complex as the cryptocurrency world, navigating the information landscape can be challenging. It's essential to follow trusted sources of information that provide accurate, well-researched, and unbiased insights. Engage with reputable news outlets, subscribe to industry-leading publications, and follow respected experts and analysts in the field. By curating your sources, you'll be better equipped to distinguish between legitimate updates and potentially misleading or sensationalized content.

One of the most enriching aspects of the cryptocurrency ecosystem is the vibrant and diverse community that surrounds it. Engage with fellow enthusiasts, investors, developers, and thought leaders through online forums, social media platforms, and industry conferences. Ask questions, engage in discussions, and share your insights.

Collaborative learning within a supportive community can provide valuable perspectives, spark innovative ideas, and foster a deeper comprehension of the challenges and opportunities that lie ahead.

While reading and researching provide foundational knowledge, hands-on experience is invaluable in understanding the intricacies of emerging technologies. Experiment with different cryptocurrencies, test out decentralized applications (DApps), and explore the functionalities of various blockchain platforms. Engaging with technologies firsthand will deepen your understanding, enabling you to grasp their potential applications and limitations more effectively.

The landscape of altcoins and emerging cryptocurrencies is marked by rapid shifts and unexpected developments. Embrace a mindset of adaptability and openness to change. Just as new technologies and projects emerge, so do unforeseen challenges and opportunities. Being adaptable allows you to pivot, learn from setbacks, and capitalize on new trends as they arise. This flexibility is crucial for making informed decisions and seizing advantageous moments in the ever-changing world of digital assets.

As you explore and learn about altcoins and emerging cryptocurrencies, remember that every investment and decision carries inherent risks and rewards. Take the time to understand the projects you're considering, assess their potential, and evaluate the associated risks. Establish a risk management strategy that aligns with your financial goals and risk tolerance. Informed decision-making will empower you to navigate the complex landscape with confidence.

As you delve into the world of digital assets, consider the ethical implications of your engagement. Recognize the potential impact of your decisions on the broader ecosystem, communities, and the environment. Engage in projects and initiatives that align with your values and contribute positively to the advancement of the technology. Ethical considerations are pivotal in shaping the responsible growth of the cryptocurrency space.

Your engagement in the cryptocurrency ecosystem can extend beyond learning and investing. Consider ways in which you can actively contribute to the community and projects that resonate with you. This could involve sharing your insights through articles, participating in open-source projects, or even collaborating on innovative solutions. By actively participating, you become an integral part of the global movement toward decentralized technologies.

The regulatory environment for cryptocurrencies is developing, and compliance is paramount. Stay updated about regulatory changes and their potential influence on the digital asset landscape. Adapting to regulatory requirements will not only ensure your investments are compliant but also contribute to the legitimacy and acceptance of cryptocurrencies in mainstream finance.

The world of altcoins and emerging cryptocurrencies is a journey that unfolds over time. Embrace a long-term perspective that values patience, perseverance, and a vision for the future. While short-term fluctuations are inevitable, focus on the underlying potential of technologies and projects. By doing so, you'll be better equipped to weather market volatility and capitalize on opportunities that align with your broader goals.

In conclusion, the exploration of altcoins and emerging cryptocurrencies is an exciting voyage that requires dedication, curiosity, and a commitment to lifelong learning. As technology evolves and paradigms shift, remaining informed and engaged will empower you to navigate the intricate landscape with confidence and wisdom. The world of digital assets holds the promise of reshaping economies, fostering inclusivity, and challenging established norms. By continuing your journey of discovery, you contribute to the ongoing evolution of this transformative space, and you stand to play a vital role in shaping the future of finance, technology, and society.

Final thoughts on the potential of altcoins and emerging cryptocurrencies

As we draw the curtains on this comprehensive exploration of altcoins and emerging cryptocurrencies, it's an opportune moment to reflect on the vast potential that this dynamic and transformative realm holds. Throughout this journey, we've delved into the intricacies of these digital assets, dissected their technological underpinnings, examined their real-world applications, and contemplated the challenges and opportunities they present. In these final thoughts, we distill the essence of our discussions, encapsulating the myriad ways in which altcoins and emerging cryptocurrencies are poised to shape the future of finance, technology, and society at large.

Altcoins and emerging cryptocurrencies are the sparks igniting a bonfire of innovation that engulfs traditional industries and reshapes the contours of our financial ecosystem. Their foundational technologies, ranging from smart contracts to novel consensus mechanisms, have the potential to revolutionize not just how we transact, but also how we govern, trade, and interact with digital systems. By offering innovative solutions to long-standing challenges, these technologies catalyze unprecedented disruption, introducing efficiencies, transparency, and security that were once thought unattainable.

At the heart of altcoins' potential lies the transformative power to democratize access to financial services and ownership. Through decentralized finance (DeFi) platforms, individuals around the globe gain the ability to participate in lending, borrowing, and trading without intermediaries. This empowers the unbanked and underbanked, providing them with opportunities to generate income and build wealth. Additionally, the fractional ownership made possible by cryptocurrencies enables a new era of asset ownership, where individuals can invest in real estate, artwork, and other traditionally illiquid assets with ease.

Beyond finance, emerging cryptocurrencies are set to reshape entire industries and supply chains. Blockchain's transparent and traceable nature can revolutionize supply chain management, ensuring authenticity, ethical sourcing, and reducing fraud. Industries from healthcare to agriculture stand to benefit from increased transparency and efficiency, resulting in more accountable practices and better consumer experiences. This transformation extends to intellectual property, where non-fungible tokens (NFTs) are revolutionizing how creators monetize and protect their digital creations.

One of the most profound promises of altcoins is the potential to foster global inclusivity and financial empowerment. These technologies transcend geographical boundaries, enabling cross-border transactions with minimal fees and delays. This has immense implications for remittances, trade, and international cooperation. Altcoins empower individuals in regions with limited access to traditional financial systems, enabling them to participate in the global economy and bypass barriers that have historically excluded them.

The landscape of altcoins and emerging cryptocurrencies thrives on collaboration and open-source innovation. Blockchain projects frequently collaborate to address shared challenges and leverage each other's strengths. The spirit of open-source development fosters an environment where ideas are freely exchanged, leading to accelerated technological advancements and the evolution of the digital asset ecosystem as a whole. This collaborative ethos echoes the internet's early days and has the potential to drive exponential growth.

While regulatory challenges persist, there is a growing recognition of the potential benefits that altcoins and cryptocurrencies bring to the financial landscape. As regulatory frameworks mature, they provide a path for mainstream adoption and institutional participation. This legitimization can instill greater confidence in investors, fostering stability and attracting traditional financial players to the digital asset arena. Moreover, regulatory clarity will facilitate the emergence of responsible projects and practices that prioritize consumer protection and security.

As the potential of altcoins becomes more evident, ethical and environmental considerations come to the forefront. The energy consumption of proof-of-work networks has prompted conversations about sustainability and the need for alternative consensus mechanisms. Similarly, the rise of NFTs has raised questions about the environmental impact of minting tokens. These considerations underline the importance of responsible innovation that aligns with the broader goals of a sustainable and inclusive future.

In the world of altcoins and emerging cryptocurrencies, we find ourselves in an uncharted terrain of possibilities. With each technological advancement, the boundaries of what can be achieved are pushed further. From decentralized autonomous organizations (DAOs) to interoperable blockchain networks, the potential for creating entirely new paradigms of governance, finance, and technology is boundless. We are at the precipice of witnessing the evolution of economic systems that prioritize fairness, inclusivity, and innovation.

As we conclude this exploration, it's imperative to embrace the journey of discovery that lies ahead. The potential of altcoins and emerging cryptocurrencies transcends individual investments; it extends to the collective transformation of our societies and economies. By staying informed, engaging in responsible practices, and contributing to the ecosystem, you become an integral part of a movement that seeks to redefine how value is exchanged, assets are owned, and transactions are conducted.

In conclusion, the potential of altcoins and emerging cryptocurrencies is a symphony of innovation, empowerment, and transformation. We stand at the crossroads of a future where financial systems are democratized, industries are revolutionized, and the very fabric of our digital interactions is reshaped. Embrace the journey with a thirst for knowledge, an openness to change, and a commitment to responsible engagement. As you navigate this ever-evolving landscape, remember that you are not just an observer, but a participant in a movement that holds the promise of a more connected, inclusive, and equitable world. The potential of altcoins and emerging cryptocurrencies is immense, and the canvas of the future is yours to shape.

Thank you for buying and reading/listening to our book. If you found this book useful/helpful please take a few minutes and leave a review on the platform where you purchased our book. Your feedback matters greatly to us.